CITY OF BIRMINGHAM
POLYTECHNIC LIBRARY

AUTHOR   CREESE, A.

TITLE   Safety for your family.

SUBJECT No.   363.13

BOOK No.

273207

P53178-B1(C)

SAFETY FOR YOUR FAMILY

BY THE SAME AUTHOR:

THE YOUNG HOMEMAKER (first and second books)

Safety for your Family

by

ANGELA CREESE

MILLS & BOON LIMITED
LONDON

First published 1968 by Mills & Boon Limited
50 Grafton Way, Fitzroy Square, London, W1

© ANGELA CREESE 1968

Reprinted 1970

SBN 263·70021·6

MADE AND PRINTED IN GREAT BRITAIN BY
THE GARDEN CITY PRESS LIMITED
LETCHWORTH, HERTFORDSHIRE

CONTENTS

	Page
THE HOME	11
Planning for safety	11
Buying for safety	25
Running the home	32
Cleaning and tidying	33
Safe cookery	39
Safe laundry	48
Sewing safely	51
Pets	52
Handyman and repairs	54
Gas	57
Electricity	62
Gardens	71
CHILDREN	74
Falls	74
Cuts, scratches, etc.	80
Electrocution	83
Poisoning	86
Scalds	92
Suffocation	96
Burns	101
Hurting little children	106
Illness	108
Play	112
Toys	116
Outdoors	120
Teaching children safety	123
OLD PEOPLE	132
Keeping old people safe	132
ACCIDENTS	141
What to do	141
Burns and scalds	143
Loss of consciousness	145
Poisoning	147
Electrocution	148
Cuts, scratches, etc.	150

Falls 150
Bites and stings 152
Varicose vein (burst) 153
Shock 153
Forms of choking, smothering, etc. 155
Person gassed 155
Person overcome by Fumes 156
Swallowed objects 156
Strangulation 157
Drowning 157
Baby smothered 158
Artificial respiration 158
Fits 160
Heat stroke 161
Body too cold 162
Eyes, ears, nose 163
Eyes 163
Ears 163
Nose 163
When to call the doctor 164
First aid box 165
MEDICINE 167
How to use medicine safely 167
SAFETY FROM ILLNESS 174
Safe food 174
Pests 187
Hygiene 189
Avoidable illnesses 199
Anxiety 200
OUTDOORS 203
Road safety 203
Walking 203
Cycling 207
Public transport 208
Driving 209
At school 216
At work 217
Safe holidays 219
"Come back safely" hints 220
Leaving home 230
FIRE 232
About fire 232
Preventing fires 233
Taking precautions 250

CRIME 259
  Protecting the house 259
  Protecting valuables 266
  Protecting children 272
  Protecting the family business 275
  The police will help 276
  Children and the law 277
USEFUL ADDRESSES 280

ACKNOWLEDGMENTS

Any writer on safety must be indebted, to a greater or less degree, to many official and semi-official publications. I should like to mention, with appreciation, those of the Royal Society for the Prevention of Accidents; the Fire Prevention Association; the British Red Cross Society; the St John Ambulance Association; the Crime Prevention Department, Essex County Constabulary; the World Health Organization (particularly Public Health Paper No 26, *Domestic Accidents*, by Professor E. Maurice Blackett).

The drawing of the louvre window on p. 12 is taken from *Hygiene in the Home* by Elisabeth Norton, published by Mills & Boon Limited, and that of the flare-free nightdress (p. 32) is adapted from a photograph by Messrs Proban Ltd.

FOREWORD

This book is intended as a book of Safety rather than a book of accidents. For this reason it has been thought fit not to include accident statistics. Can anybody visualise a thousand children burning to death?—and if they could it would be human to shrug it off as too agonising to be looked at. However, for real safety education it is necessary to have some knowledge of what accidents can happen as well as ways of preventing them and what to do in case they happen.

Safety cannot be learnt all at once. Even after the basic rules have been learnt and the environment made safe, learning must still go on in order to keep pace with modern inventions and the more general use of potentially dangerous things. For instance the increasing use of advanced mechanical aids for the housewife running the home, for the handyman doing jobs formerly left to experts and even for children whose toys become more "real" year by year.

As there are so many places where accidents can happen and such a variety of accidents, it is important that parents and others should make a proper study of the subject of safety and that children should be taught safety by example as well as precept.

This emphasis on safety has a far wider effect than may be seen at first glance. "Safety first" is no idle expression, and the homes, works and so on which are efficiently geared to safety will of necessity also be such things as clean, labour-saving and well organized, things which are too often sought after for their own sakes, sometimes with disastrous results. For instance, the common accident of somebody slipping on a mat on a well-polished floor. A clean floor is not necessarily a safe floor but a floor made safe in every way will be a clean floor. Putting Safety first, as well as preventing accidents and contributing to well-run establishments, can also bring more comfort and happiness, a lessening of anxiety and more confidence and freedom.

There is however a sadness in any safety teaching. It runs through this book as it does through others, because in spite of all the safety teaching and help available, there will still be so many people who will have serious accidents for such reasons as poverty, ill health, lack of understanding and other difficult to combat reasons. For these people, as a society we must plan as well as grieve, and as individuals, do all we can to prevent the accidents which so often lead to unhappiness, maiming and even death to the old, the sick and the lonely who live around us.

A book of this size cannot hope to cover all the possible accidents and their safety precautions. It should therefore be read, when necessary, in conjunction with specialized writings on the subject required. For instance on the subject of mountaineering more specialized information can be obtained from the British Mountaineering Council. A list of the addresses of such bodies is to be found at the end of the book.

No book can offer immunity from accident to those who read it, would that this were so, but if only one person, perhaps a little child, is saved from a serious accident because a reader of this book has become safety-conscious, then the book will have been worth writing.

A. C.

The Home

 Planning for Safety

A great many accidents can be prevented by careful home planning.

THE AREA

If you are lucky, you can start by planning **where** to live.

If there are small children in the family, parents will often put up with great inconvenience, e.g. long journeys to work, so that the family can live in an area without such dangers as busy streets, railway lines, canals, etc.

THE HOUSE

Here again, lucky people have the opportunity to plan the building of their house so that the whole building is

(*a*) Safely constructed
(*b*) Made of the safest possible materials.

Most people don't get the chance to plan whether they will live in a safe area, nor to build their homes safely, but they can usually plan for safety in such things as

(*a*) Alterations
(*b*) Lighting
(*c*) Heating
(*d*) Where to put things.

ALTERATIONS

It would be very nice to be able to go round the house looking for anything that could be altered to make the place safer, and get it all done at once. Result? Many accidents wouldn't happen.

Although most people can't do this, they can **build up safety** bit by bit. All houses have their particular danger points, but here are a few general alterations to cut down home accidents.

Louvre type window

Windows

1. Louvre type windows are probably safer than any for preventing falls from windows.

    As it would cost a lot of money to alter all the windows in the house at once, the following order would be most helpful.

    Children's rooms
    Rooms children are alone in, e.g. Bathrooms
    　　　　　　　　　　　　　　　　　Lavatories
    The rest of the upstairs windows
    Downstairs.

    Until the windows can be altered the fixing of bars (see p. 76) in children's rooms is a MUST, but they must be fixed in such a way that they can be removed by an adult in the case of fire!

2. Upstairs windows or any other windows likely to be dangerous for children could be nailed up completely and fitted with ventilating discs, or fans.

Doors

Doors can be a source of danger

1. When children can get through them to a danger area.
2. When handles stick out and catch clothes.
3. When sharp latches stick out and cut across children's faces.
4. If there are gaps at the bottom where children's fingers can get caught.
5. Where two doors open on to each other, e.g. some larder doors and back doors.
6. Where a child can get a bad bang or be knocked down as in the case of doors all made of wood or just the lower half made of wood.
7. Glass panelled doors can cause bad cutting accidents if they break.

Doors can be made safer by

1. Using armour plate glass, with guard rails or patterns.
2. Taking them off and using either sliding doors or "walk through" curtains or having no door at all in some places.
3. Using "stable doors" so that children can see and talk to Mother in the kitchen but can't get through.
4. Putting handles and locks higher up.
5. Changing handles and locks.
6. Some handymen might be able to take doors off and re-hang them like fridge doors—wide spaces at the hinge side which can be filled up with foam or soft rubber.

Steps and stairs

1. Where banisters are far apart the banister side of the stairs can be boarded in.
2. Those "one or two" steps inside and outside the house are very dangerous to old people. In some cases it will be safer to replace these with a ramp (i.e. make the ground slope—but this would still need a banister).
3. An extra hand rail can easily be fitted on the wall side of the staircase.
4. Gates at top and bottom of stairs can easily be fitted too.

LIGHTING

Many people spend a lot of time, trouble and money on planning decorative lighting schemes which often make the house look lovely but are not always SAFE.

The way to plan is to plan for SAFETY first and then for effect. Most older houses do not have enough lights and many new houses don't have lights where they would prevent accidents.

To be really safe, there should be:

(*a*) No dark or half-dark spots in the day time
(*b*) No part of the house which cannot be safely lit up at night
(*c*) No glare and no dark shadows.

"Half lights" can be very restful sometimes, but they should never be used:

(*a*) On stairs and landings as the only lighting.
(*b*) Where work is going on and where accidents could happen if the worker can't see properly.
(*c*) Where there are very old people. Even in a sitting room a very old person may trip over something if the light is dim.

It should be possible to have good light:

(*a*) In every room.
(*b*) In halls.
(*c*) On landings.
(*d*) On stairs or where there are just one or two steps.
(*e*) Outside the back door—particularly if there are steps.
(*f*) Outside the front door—particularly if there are steps or a separate porch.
(*g*) In outside lavatories and any outside buildings likely to be used when it is dark.

Extra lights are needed

1. In deep cupboards, especially where heavy things are stored.
2. In cellars.
3. In dark corners.
4. Where stairs turn round.
5. An extra light on top landings (or halls in some cases) which is separate from the main light for the area.

    This extra light should have a low wattage bulb in it so that it can be kept on all night.

    This is very handy for anyone who has to get up at night, particularly if there are babies or old people in the house.

    Having this low light makes it easy to find the switch for the main light too.
6. Some houses have spots which are half-dark even in the day-time. If a window can't be put in, a low wattage lamp burning all day is the answer.

Light   →

A front-door light makes steps safer and may discourage burglars

Switches

(*a*) It should be possible to switch all lights on from the top and the bottom of the stairs.

(*b*) Room and hall switches should be just inside the door. Sometimes people get them fitted outside the door, which is often better still.

Ring Circuit

This is the modern method of installing electricity in a house. It is much more convenient and safer than the old way. As the general installation is the householder's responsibility (apart from the meters) it is a good idea to change to the ring circuit system if you get the chance. Get the local Electricity Board to do the job.

HEATING

As many fires and burns are caused directly or indirectly by the home heating system it is of the utmost importance to plan the heating system first of all for SAFETY.

If it is your own house which has to be heated, what may be your safest system is often made more possible nowadays by monthly payments schemes.

In flats and rented houses you can usually only plan to make the existing system as safe as possible.

Planning for a new system

If you can plan which heating system you want, the things to consider, apart from money, are:

1. What are the chances of somebody getting burnt or otherwise hurt from it?
2. What are the chances of
    (a) It setting fire to the house
    (b) Somebody using it and setting fire to the house.

3. How safe it is:
    (a) If you are tired or not well
    (b) If children or old people use it
    (c) If you do something wrong.

    Has it **built in** safety, i.e. is it "FAIL SAFE"?

The best thing to do is:

1. Get to know as much as you can about all the heating systems.
2. Ask the above questions about each one.
3. Decide which is the SAFEST. (Forget about money while you decide.)

Then, move heaven and earth to find a way to get the system which is safest for your family and your home.

Planning safety for the not so safe system

You will have to do this if you just can't get the system which you feel is safest, or if the one you have is not very safe but you can't alter it.

Some hints are:

1. Do your best to make sure the actual burning parts can't be touched.
    (a) Use strong, fine-meshed, well-fixed fire guards.
    (b) Put the appliance where people don't have to keep passing it.

2. Make sure the surrounding area is safe, e.g.

    (*a*) No worn mats to trip over
    (*b*) No cotton rugs to flare up if an accident does happen
    (*c*) No source of draught.

3. Plan a safe place to keep the fuel.
4. Plan who is going to be mainly responsible for looking after it.

When you are trying to prevent accidents happening from something which is not really safe to start with, e.g.

An open fire in a house **made** of much inflammable material and **full** of many inflammable materials—

as well as planning for safety when you first go to live in the place you have to take **constant care** to prevent accidents happening. This does not mean being in a state of constant anxiety!

WHERE TO PUT THINGS

If this is planned properly to start with, and checked every now and again as time goes on, all kinds of accidents can be prevented. Planning should aim at:

1. Keeping "traffic lanes" clear
2. Keeping danger spots clear
3. Leaving plenty of "room to move"
4. Providing plenty of easy to get at storage space
5. Putting things where it won't be dangerous to get to them, e.g. meters too high or too low.

"Traffic lanes"

These include:

1. All passages and stairways
2. Routes most often used in rooms, e.g.

    From door to fire
    From door to windows
    From door to bed or armchairs
    From door to table.

Every home has its "traffic lanes" and these can easily be noted, e.g. it would be dangerous to have to step over an electric fire every time the television needed to be adjusted—either the television or the fire should be moved.

Danger spots

For most homes these are:

1. The tops of stairs
2. Under windows
3. By unguarded fires
4. Behind doors.

If things are placed near any of these danger spots then accidents like this will happen:

People will fall down stairs.
Children will climb on whatever is under the window, e.g. a table, and fall out of the window.
People will fall into the fireplace.
People will bang their heads on doors when the door is prevented from opening properly by the thing behind it.

The best thing to do is to:

(a) Go round the house and note the danger spots.
(b) Make sure no furniture which could cause an accident is put near one of these danger places.

Room to move

More space means less accidents.
How to get it?

1. Don't waste it
2. Use all you have
3. Make more.

Wasting space

Space can be wasted very easily by:

1. Not planning how it is to be used.
2. Having too many things in a room.
3. Arranging furniture, etc., badly.
4. Not putting things away after use.
5. Not having enough storage space.

Using space

1. Don't put big things where they "take up all the space", not leaving enough for safe movement.
2. Don't put little things in a space which could take something larger.
3. Leave as much space in the middle of the room as possible.

4. Buy things the right size

    (*a*) For the size of the room

    (*b*) For the alcove, etc. you want them to fit.

"Double-up" where possible:

1. Use furniture which does at least two jobs, e.g.

    Bed chairs and settees
    Beds with drawers underneath
    Vanitory units—dressing table and wash basin in one.

2. Use rooms for at least two purposes, e.g.

    Kitchen—diners
    Lounge—diners
    Bed—sitting rooms. Most bedrooms are just wasted space
    all day!

    Where people have very little room, even the passage gets
used for meals. To do this safely a flap table fitted to the wall,
which can be let down when not in use, is best.

Make the most of "odd" spaces: e.g. tuck things under.

    The space under the stairs if fitted with shelves will hold more
than just throwing things in.
    Dining sets with chairs and stools made to slide under.
    Nests of tables etc.

But don't overdo the "tucking under" or things will get left out.
Put things on top:

    Sets of shelves on chests, desks, etc.
    Make sure they are safe—fasten them to the wall. (Don't go
too high!)

Use the corners:

    Corner shelves are useful for any room.

Use the doors:

    Put long shelves (with rims) on the back of larder doors for
small jars, etc.
    Fix shelves or curtain rails to back of wardrobe or cupboard
doors to hold ties, etc., etc.

Use the walls:

    All kinds of shelves and cupboards can be fixed to walls but
make sure they

(a) Are firmly fixed.

(b) Don't go too high!

Other hints for using space are to buy:

1. Stacking furniture—chairs and tables. Café furniture is **made** to save space.
2. "Growing" furniture—this is doubly useful

   (a) It fits together neatly and doesn't waste space.

   (b) It can be re-arranged to save space anywhere.

3. Folding furniture—chairs, beds, tables, **but** make sure they are always set up safely.
4. "Mobile" furniture—handy to push back to the wall or in a corner after use, e.g. tea trolleys, book-case trolleys, sideboards, etc.
5. "Built-in" furniture—really means making the room smaller but leaves more space in the middle of the room.

Making space:

General ways are:

1. Laying a proper floor in the loft to make use of roof space.
2. Building rooms in the loft.
3. Building extensions on to the house.
4. Making rooms larger by adding on passage space, etc.
5. Using sliding doors or "walk through" curtains.

Models and Plans

These are a great help to using space well. The models can be:

An accurate model of the room with scaled-down size model furniture

or Just a cardboard scaled-down pattern of the floor, marking alcoves, etc.

Then furniture, etc., can be placed

(a) To save space

(b) To keep "traffic lanes" clear.

"Stacking and storing"

Every home needs lots and lots of storage space which should be:

(a) Easy to get at

(b) Properly used

(c) Near to where the job is done, e.g. a place for records **in the**

room where the record player is used and better still **near** to where it is used.

(d) Properly laid out, e.g. with enough shelves or drawers of the right width and depth and height.

(e) Kept tidy.

Different kinds of storage space will usually be needed, e.g.

Open shelves
Closed cupboards or shelves
Locking cupboards and drawers.

They can be either:

Fixed to walls
Stand on the floor
Be on small wheels or castors.

Locks—One of the chief jobs which should be included in safety planning is fixing locks or difficult-to-open fastenings to all drawers, cupboards and doors which **contain** things dangerous to small children or would be dangerous for children to **get into**. These include:

Medicine and First Aid boxes as already noted.
Cupboards or drawers where "beauty" things are kept.
Fridges and deep freezes
Central heating boilers
Cocktail cabinets
Sewing boxes
Cleaning cupboards
Larders
Garages and sheds
Coal cellars,
etc., etc.

This is not as easy as it sounds because some things which are sold without safe fasteners are very difficult for a handyman to fix them on to.

THE KITCHEN

When kitchens are being planned either from the beginning or bit by bit, everything must be planned firstly for SAFETY, then for appearance, etc.

This is no easy job because:

(a) The kitchen is often built in an unsafe way to start with.

(*b*) Much of the fixed equipment is not in the safest position.

(*c*) Kitchens are often too small or too large.

How to plan a kitchen for safety—if you get the chance.

Most of what has already been written in this section and other sections for making the home a safe place applies to kitchens too, but here are a few extra points to check up on.

Lighting—Extra lights may be needed over sink, cooker, and work tables. A deep larder or other cupboard would need a light too.

Power points—Where electricity is the main fuel, check with Electricity Board to find out how many you need for safety.

Ventilation—Good ventilation is important in a kitchen, particularly if gas is used. It also helps to cut down fatigue, which is the cause of many accidents. If open windows cause a draught, advice should be got on the best form of artificial ventilation.

"Traffic lanes"—Ideally, people should not be able to pass between the cooker and sink, or between any other two places where hot pans, liquids, etc. may be carried.

Placing equipment—(*a*) No equipment should be placed where it can be knocked by the door. Sliding doors help here.

(*b*) Beware of the handyman who puts up shelves or wall cupboards where anybody can bang their heads on them!

DANGEROUS

(*c*) Cookers or boiling tops should not be placed near a possible draught. This means either moving the cooker etc., or changing the type of ventilation.

(*d*) Cookers should not have their sides against a wall. If there is nowhere else to put them it's a help if they can be made movable. Then they can be moved at least a few inches from the wall.

(*e*) Heavy pans, etc. should not be kept on high shelves—partly because it's difficult to lift heavy things down from high places—and partly because if they fall somebody may get badly hurt.

(*f*) Any cupboards or shelves fixed to walls **must** be fixed very firmly.

Doors—All doors should have enough space so that they can be opened safely.

Otherwise, take them off, using sliding doors, or in the case of a cooker in an awkward position a drop door would be safer.

Floors—It is most important that they should be in good condition and non-slip when wet.

Working surfaces—(*a*) All surfaces and equipment should be at a convenient height to work at or accidents will happen because the worker hasn't got complete freedom of movement or uses a piece of wood, etc., to stand on.

(*b*) If possible all working surfaces should be of the same height, or things will get knocked as they are moved to the higher surface or fall down on to a lower one.

(*c*) Working surfaces should be big enough, or things will keep falling off—dangerous in the case of hot liquids, etc.

Room to move—This is very important in a kitchen but nearly impossible in some!

The best that can be done is to

(*a*) Place everything round the walls
(*b*) Put things away at once after use, e.g. washing machines.
(*c*) Keep other people out! Pets too if you can.

"Good working sequence"—This means being able to go from one working place to the next in the order the job is being done, e.g. preparing, cooking, serving, washing up, putting away.

This is a convenient and safe way of working for some people but other people like "dodging about".

The best thing is for each family to work out the best kitchen working sequence for themselves in the kitchen they have.

Danger spots in kitchens—These are usually caused by such things as:

Too hot water coming from the tap
Wet or greasy floors
Not enough **easy to get at** storage space
Too many people in the kitchen at once

Children and pets underfoot
etc.

How to get rid of danger spots?

   1. First of all make a note of them.
   2. Plan how to get rid of them or lessen them, e.g.

     (*a*) Alter where you can
     (*b*) Fix safety devices where possible
     (*c*) Take constant care
     (*d*) Make strict kitchen rules.

 # Buying for Safety

Any things bought for the house or personal use will be SAFER if they are:

Well designed
Made of good materials
Made of SAFE materials
Made properly
The right size and weight for the user
Easy to move if necessary.

The following do much to make sure that the things we use **are** safe:

The British Standards Institute
Acts of Parliament
The Council of Industrial Design
The Consumer Council
Gas Boards
Electricity Boards
Many manufacturers who take trouble to make things safe.
Many shopkeepers who do their best to stock safe goods.

The next step is up to the SHOPPER to:

(*a*) Buy the SAFEST things they can find.
(*b*) Report anything dangerous in the things they buy to:

     Citizens Advice Bureau
     The Consumer Council

(c) Take trouble to find out the latest safety devices for general use.

(d) Look out for any safety equipment or devices meant for very young, very old, or disabled people.

Many of these things would be very useful for keeping the rest of the family safe, e.g.

Bath rails—**anybody** can slip in the bath!

(e) To find out as much as they can about the article **before** buying it, e.g.

Ask   —what happens if anything goes wrong?
      Is there a safety valve—such as a cut-out switch in electrical goods?
      Is it poisonous, explosive, etc?

Look —For SAFETY labels such as:

      The B.S.I. KITE MARK
      The Gas Board's safety label
      The Electricity Board's safety label

      For—Danger points
      For—Safety points.

Test   —Ask to see it working.
      Work it yourself.

Think—Will it be safe in your house?
      Is there a safe place for it?
      Is there anybody who is sure to get hurt by it?

Here are a few extra points to look for before buying things.

The House

(a) Look for BUILT-IN safety, e.g. if there aren't any dark corners on stairs you don't have to make them safe!

(b) Look at it from the point of view of those who will live in it, e.g. is it safe for little children, old people, anybody blind or disabled who will live there.

(c) Look for danger points outside and inside, e.g. too steep stairs. Ask yourself—can you afford to make any dangerous point safe? If you can't, then the family is already sentenced to certain accidents.

Furniture

Must be strongly made, especially where there are children.

Must stand firm—even some arm chairs tip up!
Must move easily—when you want them to!
Have no sharp corners—rounded ones are safer.
Have no rough edges—check underneath and behind.
Make sure that drawers and doors open and close properly.
Check that mirrors are fixed firmly.
Look for—B.S.I. numbers, KITE mark, Design Centre labels, etc.
Buy things the right height.

Signs to look for on goods you buy

Electric goods

Look for the Electrical Approval Mark of the B.E.A.B. and for B.S. numbers.

Look for automatic safety cut-outs.

Look for the mark which shows the appliance is double insulated (overleaf).

This is the sign of a double insulated appliance

Check with a qualified electrician before buying electrical goods from other countries.

Think—whether it's safe enough for you and your family.

Be careful to buy shades big enough for light bulbs, so that they will not catch fire. Look for safety materials too.

Cookers—radiant plates are best—you can **see** when they are on. Test cookers all over for sharp edges.

Gas appliances

Look for the Gas Board's safety sign.

Gas fires—flat tops tempt people to put clothes, papers, etc. on them.

Cookers—look out for safety valves which cut out gas supply when burners don't light.

Test all over for sharp edges.

Oil stoves

Look for B.S.I. numbers and KITE mark.

Check for yourself whether even a "safe" oil stove would be safe for your home.

Look for non-spill oil cans.

Buying secondhand

Check for safety in every way you can think of, especially in portable fires.

Repairs

Electric —Electricity Board or other qualified electricians.
Gas —Gas Board for most jobs.
For some jobs they will recommend approved fitters.

All other jobs—Go for the qualified man.
Go for members of Trade Associations.
If you don't know whether there is a Trade Association for a particular job, ask—

Citizens Advice Bureaux
Consumer Council
Public Libraries (Reference Dept).

Furniture (secondhand)—look for dry rot or any other weakness—the thing may collapse.

China and Glass

Look for these safety points:

Good balance
Easy to hold
Stack firmly
Unbreakable ware for children and "butter-fingers"
Teapots, coffee pots must—pour well
have well fitting lids
have handles that don't get too hot.

Cutlery

Knives —with handles which won't come off
—Sharp enough for the job
Forks —No sharp points
Carving sets—Strong guards.

Cooking utensils—Safety points are:

Well fitting lids
Handles which don't get hot
Good balance
Glass pans with handles that come off may be safer where there are toddlers.
"Rough" feeling handles are safer than smooth shiny ones.

Not too heavy for general use.
Easy to hold.
Well fitting lids.
Dishes which can be changed from hot to cold (and back again)
    safely.
Can openers which don't leave ragged edges.

Fire guards

Look for British Standard numbers—
for solid fuel fire guards
for solid fuel combustion grate guards.

Plastics

Look for B.S. numbers for these, which mean no fire risk, e.g. on
some lampshades.

Christmas decorations

Choose those which are "non-flare" and "melt-proof".

Soft furnishings

Look for "non-flare" material, e.g.

Curtains   —Terylene melts but doesn't flare up.
                Cotton—look for "flame-resistant" finish
                Fibre glass—won't flare up.
                Velvet—look for the flame-resistant kind.
Sheets, etc.—Terylene is safer than cotton, winceyette or cotton
                twill, for example.

Hearthrugs

Go all out for "non-flare" ones.
Beware home-made ones made out of odd scraps of material.
Look for non-slip rugs always.

Bedside lamps

Must have a firm base.

Solid fuel

Smokeless fuel is safer.

Bolts for lavatory and bathroom doors

Look out for indicator bolts which open from both sides.

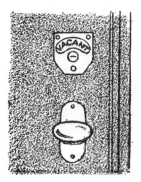

An indicator bolt for bathrooms and toilets

Left-handed?

More things are made for left-handed people than some realise. Ask for them in the shops, write to manufacturers too.

Buying for children

Look for safety all the time, e.g.:

"Safe from fire" —"non-flare" materials, e.g. Proban, for clothes, cot drapes, etc.

"Safe from falls" —shoes, harnesses, trousers, etc. not too large.

"Safe when alone" —inter-com systems.

"Safe when asleep"—safety pillows, bars to prevent falling out of bed, etc.

"Safe in the bath" —special bath seats.

Trousers, anoraks and "all-in-one" suits are safer than dresses and long coats.

Note

Noise upsets some people and can cause accidents. Therefore buy with a view to cutting down noise as much as possible.

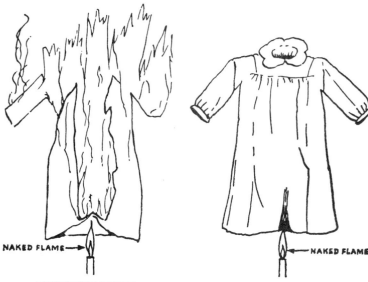

NAKED FLAME →

← NAKED FLAME

UNTREATED FABRIC
THE NIGHTDRESS IS TOTALLY CONSUMED
WITHIN 15 SECONDS OF BEING EXPOSED
TO A NAKED FLAME

PROBAN FINISHED FABRIC
THE GARMENT DOES NOT BLAZE,
ALTHOUGH IT IS IN DIRECT
CONTACT WITH THE FLAME

Running the Home

Most housewives have so much to do in a set time that accidents seem bound to happen.

Many of these accidents are serious enough to mean loss of life or serious injury.

An even larger number of accidents happen which don't cause any great harm but they do get people **used** to having accidents, which makes more serious accidents more likely to occur.

Everything should be done to cut down not only the number of serious accidents but also the large number of lesser accidents which occur in the running of a home.

Here are some ways to do it:

CLEANING AND TIDYING

USE THE BEST METHOD

In housework this is often discovered by trial and error.
A better way is to:

(a) Find out the correct and safest method
(b) Practise until it becomes a habit.

This is particularly important when using equipment which may
be dangerous, e.g.

Electric things
Knives, tin openers, etc.
Anything using heat
Anything using hot water
Anything to do with children

Using the best method often saves time too, which means not
having to hurry so much, which again cuts down accidents.

PLAN TIME

This is more difficult to do, partly because time has to be found
in the first place to do the planning and partly because every now
and again the situation changes, e.g. when a new baby arrives.
Hints on how to plan time:

1. Don't do so much

(a) Get as much help as possible, e.g. get somebody in to help, or
    share jobs round the family.
        Don't forget children must be shown how to do jobs safely.
(b) Send work out, e.g. to laundries, cleaners, etc.
(c) Leave it sometimes.

2. Make the work easy

(a) Use labour-saving equipment.
(b) Use quick cleaners for floor, windows, silver, etc.
(c) Buy easy care materials for curtains, sheets, etc.
(d) Use electricity or gas instead of coal and oil if possible.
(e) Shop when the shops aren't busy.
(f) Get things sent if possible.

3. Work out

(a) How long jobs take

(*b*) What jobs **must** be done
(*c*) Which jobs you needn't do
(*d*) How much time you have and when.

4. Make work plans

An easy way to do this is:

(*a*) Divide the day into blocks of time, e.g.
from getting up to getting everybody off.
(*b*) Note the "rush" periods, e.g.
early morning, lunch time, etc.
(*c*) Fit in rest times, e.g.
after lunch, after tea.

5. Big jobs

e.g. Decorating—plan these well ahead to save too much dis-organization of the daily routine of the house.

6. Oiling the wheels

There are many ways of doing this so that time and temper are saved and accidents cut down.
Here are some:

(*a*) Regularity—have set times and days to do regular jobs.
(*b*) The Right Time—all kinds of panic and rushing can be saved if at least one clock or watch in the house always gives the correct time.
(*c*) "A place for everything and everything in its place." This is important for saving time and vital for accident prevention, e.g. in the case of sharp knives, medicines, etc.

7. Routine is important

Apart from time saving, regular meal times, bed times, etc., a good routine means that things can be planned ahead, toys etc. can be tidied away before bed time, people get less tired. These are all things which cut down the causes of accidents.

DRESS FOR THE JOB

This is just as important for the prevention of accidents in the home as in factories and workshops.
Loose flowing clothes and apron strings catch on door handles.
Big pockets and long chain necklaces catch pan handles, etc.
Torn hems can be very dangerous too.

Tight clothes prevent free movement.

Shoes: loose shoes, high-heeled shoes, old slippers, can all be dangerous. Well fastened, low-heeled shoes properly soled and heeled are safer. Shoes with composition soles are often very very slippery on wet floors.

USE AND CARE OF EQUIPMENT

All household equipment must be properly installed, checked regularly and repaired as soon as possible by qualified people.

It must also:

Be safe
Be strong for the job
Be right for the job
Work properly

Proper care of equipment includes:

Using it properly for the right purpose
Caring for it, e.g. cleaning, oiling, etc.
Storing it carefully.

Small repairs

Small repair jobs not done properly can cost lives (see also p. 54)·

While doing the housework it is a good idea to make a note to get these small repair jobs done at once or replace the article, e.g.

Loose pan handles
Sticking doors, windows, drawers
Loose stair rods, bits of lino, etc.
Blunt knives
Tin openers that won't work properly
Loose plugs, switches and other small electrical faults, etc.

WAYS OF WORKING

1. Climbing jobs

(a) Strong steps are best but a strong chair is next best.
(b) Long-handled brushes save a lot of climbing.

2. Cleaning equipment

(a) Get out only what you need for the job.
(b) Mind where you leave it while working.
(c) Put it away as soon as you have finished with it.

Use strong steps for climbing, or . . .

3. Don't strain yourself

(*a*) Sit for as many jobs as possible.

(*b*) When standing, at the sink, table, stove, etc., stand firmly on both feet.

(*c*) Try not to overstretch in any direction.

(*d*) Walk properly—slouching is tiring.

(*e*) Picking up heavy things:

Bend knees slightly
Get a good grip on the object
Then lift
Lifting things in the wrong way causes strained backs as well as many accidents.
Get help to move heavy or awkward things.

... a long-handled brush may save climbing

4. Use your brains

Think up ways to save work and to make it easier, e.g.

Use trolleys and trays when tidying up.
Use boxes and buckets to carry cleaning things.
Keep some cleaning things upstairs—in a safe place of course.
Soak clothes, pans, parts of gas stoves to make cleaning easier.

USING CLEANING MATERIALS SAFELY

The first rule to be remembered about cleaning materials is to reckon that they are all poisonous if eaten or drunk.

General rules for using them safely are:

1. Never use bleach and lavatory cleaner together. This mixture gives off dangerous fumes. It's safer not to mix any cleaning materials together if you don't know what may happen.
2. Flammable cleaners. See p. 244.
3. Every cleaning material must be kept in a safe place. Only have the bottle or tin in use out, and when finished with put it away where children can't get at it. (Lid on.) "Safe places" have to be thought out very carefully for each home. "Under the sink" is not safe if children can get at it.
4. Try to keep all labels and directions clean. Re-label if necessary.
5. READ directions when you get stuff home from the shop, then you know if it needs to be put away safely.
6. NEVER put any cleaning materials or other dangerous thing in a bottle or tin which is made for food or drink, e.g. in lemonade bottles, etc.
7. DON'T use cleaning containers to put other cleaners in.
8. NEVER keep jars, bottles, etc. which have contained things which may be poison, however nice the bottle, etc. is, e.g. home perm bottles. Throw them away at once.

   (*a*) There may still be a little in it.
   (*b*) A child may drink out of a bottle which is full of, say, perming fluid, etc. sometime.

9. Take extra care with any insect sprays where there are small children.
10. Don't use more cleaner than is really necessary. A quick wipe over the inside of the oven after each use and you never have to use oven cleaners at all.
11. Use the correct cleaner for the job, e.g. some modern floor coverings can be very dangerous if you use the wrong cleaner on them. Ask at the shop for safety.

Note

1. Be extra careful with:

   (*a*) Cleaning liquids which **look** like something a child often has, e.g.
      Disinfectant which looks like orange juice.
   (*b*) Cleaning liquids which come in similar shaped bottles to something a child often has, e.g.
      Rose Hip syrup bottles and disinfectant bottles.
   (*c*) Pretty coloured cleaners, e.g. pink ones.

2. NEVER give small children empty cleaning material containers to play with. They may play with full ones sometime!

RUBBISH. See also p. 241

Many unnecessary accidents are caused because rubbish is left in the house.

Safety hints are:

1. Never put dangerous rubbish in pedal bins where children can get at it.
2. Put these things straight into the dustbin—

    All containers which have had poisonous things in them.
    All cleaning containers
    All empty food tins (wrap well first).
    All broken glass (wrap well first).
    All other broken things which can't be mended (wrap well if sharp).
    Any very old food from the larder.
    Empty aerosols
    Anything which may be dangerous to anybody if left in the house.

3. Keep dustbins out of reach of small children if possible. A strong well fitting lid will help to keep small children out.
4. Tell the dustman if you put glass in the dustbin.

SAFE COOKERY

The most usual accidents likely to happen whilst cooking are:

BURNS AND SCALDS
CUTS
SLIPPING ON THE FLOOR

The main ways to prevent these accidents when cooking are pretty well the same as when doing housework, i.e.

Using the best method
Becoming skilled at the job
Using good safe equipment which is right for the job
Using and caring for equipment properly
Planning work and time
Dressing for the job
Working tidily and cleanly.

Special safety measures include:

Making extra sure that electrical equipment is safe

Being extra careful with electrical equipment when water is about
Having good lighting and ventilation (see pp. 15, 23).
Not having too many people around when cooking is being done.

USING THE COOKER

General safety rules include:

Keeping it clean
Turning parts off when finished with
Never let anybody use it for other things, e.g. chemistry experiments.

Keeping all safety rules regarding children, e.g.

Pan handles not sticking out
Safety taps
Pan guards
   etc.

The grill

(a) Don't leave it unattended when alight—food can flare up dangerously.
(b) Eye-level grills:

    Take care with long-handled grill pans, they can poke you in the eye. Don't leave them under the grill when not in use.
    Never put the oven cloth on top of the grill—one day it might be on. Result? Fire.

Gas rings and hotplates

(a) Wipe up boiled-over food at once (check gas is still burning properly afterwards). Turn off electricity before cleaning.
(b) Keep the outlet holes of gas rings clean.
(c) Don't put the oven cloth on the cooker.
(d) When trying not to leave pan handles sticking out, don't leave them over the heater of another burner either!
(e) Best not to wear metal bracelets, they can get very hot and burn the skin.
(f) Take care when stretching across to back burners if front ones are on.

Using the oven

(a) Glass doors—remember these get very hot too.
(b) Glass dishes—don't take them out of a hot oven and put them in a cold or wet place. Put them on top of the cooker or on a

folded cloth or on a pot stand or chopping board on the table.

(c) Don't put hot dishes out of the oven on the edge of the cooker or table.

Chef's trick—put salt on the lids of dishes which have just come out of the oven, to show they are hot.

(d) Bend down before opening the oven door and keep face well away from the opening. Good idea to only open it an inch to let the first rush of hot air out. It can be very dangerous if this rushes into the eyes.

(e) Drop doors—don't leave these open, especially with hot dishes and tins on them.

> Legs can be burnt
> Toddlers will touch the door and dishes.

(f) Lights in ovens save accidents.

Lighting the oven

(a) Using strips of paper is dangerous

> May start a fire
> Children may copy and get burned to death.

DANGER!

(b) Matches—Never leave them on the stove.
Don't put used ones back in the box.

Keep a jam jar of water near the stove for used matches.

(c) Lighters—If these are fixed on a long tube, be careful not to shut the tube in the oven door.

This kind of lighter is unsafe where there are small children. They may use them and start a fire.

(d) Automatic lighting

'Make sure the pilot is kept alight
Make sure jets have lit before leaving them.

(e) Battery lighters—These are safest but—

Don't leave them on the cooker top.

DANGER—don't leave a battery lighter on the stove

COOKING WITH FAT

Fat fires can happen very quickly and get out of control in no time. By taking special care when using fat, most accidents can be avoided.

Deep frying

(a) Always have the pan less than half full of fat.
(b) Don't leave it when it's heating or once it's hot.
(c) Don't have kettles boiling or lids off pans while cooking with

deep fat, in case water spills into the fat and causes spitting.

(d) Put food in and take it out gently.

(e) Never put wet food in deep fat. Dry it first, e.g. on a tea towel.

(f) Don't put too much food in the pan at once.

(g) Never over-heat the fat.

Don't wait for a haze to appear when using oil or some new fats. By the time the haze appears the fat will be far too hot.

(h) Don't put a lid on when frying in deep fat.

(i) Only strong deep pans with a firm base should be used for deep fat frying. The pan base should not be smaller than the hot plates.

(j) Turn the heat off as soon as cooking is finished.

Shallow fat frying

(a) Don't let the fat get too hot or it will splutter everywhere, on you, on a child's face or on to another flame.

(b) Choose a deep frying pan if possible.

(c) Some people find frying pans with lids are safer.

Grilling

Don't use a grill pan full of fat. Empty it and wash it each time after use.

In the oven

(a) When basting meat—take the tin right out of the oven to baste. Using a lid or foil saves basting.

(b) Don't put too much fat in tins.

Never leave packets of fat or bottles of oil on, or near, the stove. Always put the top on the oil bottle.

Never leave spilled fat on the stove or on the floor. Wipe it up quickly.

Notes

1. It is always dangerous to cook on a stove not meant for cooking, e.g.

   Oil stoves
   Gas fires
   Electric fires.

2. Cooking on barbecues indoors is dangerous.

3. Any table cooking, trolley cooking, etc., needs extra care.

4. If you wear glasses, anti-steam preparations can save accidents.

DON'T BE PUSHED FOR TIME

Cooking in a hurry means less attention to safety and more accidents.

If you know time is short, or something has gone wrong, fall back on any quick method you can think of to save having to rush to get the job done the long way.

Here are some time saving hints:

1. Don't cook, have a meal now and again that doesn't need cooking.
2. Plan meals so that one day's cooking helps the next, e.g. make enough pastry for two days.
3. Shop carefully so that you have all the things you need when you start cooking.
4. Prepare food ahead, e.g. the whole dish or just cook the meat (cool it quickly and put it in the fridge).
5. Grate cheese, cut rind off bacon, make up pastry mixes (don't add water).
6. Prepare extras and put in jars, e.g. browned bread crumbs, cake decorations, chop up cherries, angelica, nuts, etc.

Use quick methods

1. Grate—onions, carrots, apples, hard margarine.
2. Cut—things smaller to cook quicker, e.g. potatoes in half-inch slices, shred cabbage, cut meat up small for stewing.
3. Partly boil food—e.g. potatoes before roasting, rice on top of stove, then in oven.
4. Use quick flavours—e.g. stock cubes, soups, etc.
5. Small sizes—cook quicker, e.g. Yorkshire puddings, meat pies, steamed puddings, etc.
6. Work—tidily.
7. Use—time-saving tools, sharp knives, tin openers which work, etc.
8. Use—ready prepared foods from the shop when time is really short.
9. Automatic timers—mean you can prepare and cook food well beforehand.
10. Fridges and deep freezes save shopping time and mean you can prepare food, even cook it, before you need it.

CUTTING TOOLS

All cutting tools are dangerous, especially to small children. It is most important to:

Keep them away from small children
Use them correctly
Put them away after use.

Careful use and keeping of knives cannot be too strongly stressed.

DON'T leave or carry knives this way

Always:

1. Keep cooking knives sharp.
2. Cut away from yourself.
3. Cut down rather than across.
4. Keep the hand holding the food well away from the blade.
5. Keep hands behind cutting edge.
6. Use a chopping board—helps to prevent slipping.
7. Put knives at the back of the table when not using. Never leave points hanging over the edge of the table.
8. Clean, wash and dry with the back edge of the knife towards the hand.
9. Keep knives separate in the cutlery drawer and all round the same way. A higher, safer storing place is better for very sharp knives, and also if children can open drawers.

10. When carrying knives, always carry them at your side, point to the floor.

HOT WATER

General information, see pp. 48, 92

Extra rules:

1. Never lift saucepans or kettles with wet or greasy hands.
2. Never have hot water for general use (coming out of the tap) higher than 60°C.
3. Never add boiling water from a kettle whilst somebody is washing up or washing clothes, it is always dangerous. Hands and forearms can get badly scalded.
4. Never stretch over pans or kettles of boiling water—steam scalds badly too.
5. Don't use boiling water unless you really need to.
6. Water in washing up machines is extremely hot. Be careful.

Note

When pouring any hot liquids, e.g. tea, soup, etc., don't put the cups or bowls on the edge of the table. If you put them further back and there is an accident, most of the hot liquid will go on the table instead of down your legs or on children's heads.

PROTECTION

(a) Loose clothes, apron strings, and big pockets can catch on pan handles, gas taps, etc.

(b) Thin shoes and shoes without toes are not safe because they give no protection from scalds, or heavy things falling on them.

(c) Oven gloves or oven cloths should always be used. Never get things out of the oven with tea towels or the apron you are wearing or by pulling jumper sleeves down over your hands.

(d) Wash oven gloves and cloths sometimes. Very greasy ones can catch fire easily.

(e) Make sure the forearm is protected when reaching across the cooker top or into the oven, but, no loose sleeves—they might catch fire or catch on pans.

(f) Always use kettle holders when lifting kettles or pan handles which get hot.

CLEAN TIDY WORKING is always SAFER, e.g.

(a) Keeping the cooker and working surfaces clean.

(b) Getting out all the ingredients and utensils which you need to start with.

(c) Putting away things when finished with.

(d) Washing up as you go along.

(e) Floors—wipe up any spills at once. Pick up any bits of onion, potato, apple peel, bits of greasy paper.

(f) Larder—keep everything tidy, spotless and properly labelled.

CHILDREN, PETS, AND TALKERS

DANGER!

Children—(a) Are safest kept out of the kitchen if possible, at least when cooking is being done.

(b) Care must be taken all the time to keep dangerous things out of their reach.

(c) Never go away and leave a child in the kitchen

whilst electrical equipment is working, e.g. mixers, etc. Safer to take the plug out too.

Pets —Safest to keep them out if you can. This is more difficult if they are fed in the kitchen.

Talkers —Keep these out too, if you can! They distract attention, make you forget what you are doing. May even make you turn round quickly, and cause a really bad accident.

SAFE LAUNDRY

The main accidents likely to happen whilst doing the laundry are:

Scalds
Electrocution
Slipping on wet floors
Tripping over flexes and cables
Accidents to children (see p. 95)
Clothes, arms, hair, catching in washing machines.

SCALDS

Although water from the kitchen tap should not be hot enough to scald, water used in washing and washing up equipment needs to be hotter.

Extra care to prevent scalds should be taken when using:

Washing machines
Boilers

Notes

(a) Always remember that STEAM scalds too, Keep face and arms away when opening equipment.

(b) If using kettles of boiling water for small washes, be careful where you put the kettle down—children may get scalded. Anybody may trip over the kettle and get scalded.

(c) Never fill boilers too full—they will boil over scalding water.

(d) Be extra careful when using small boilers, large saucepans, bowls, etc. on stoves. Don't leave them alone when they are boiling.

(e) Always use strong laundry tongs when taking clothes out of boiling water.

Taking clothes out with wooden spoons, odd sticks or finger-tips is always dangerous.

ELECTRICITY

It cannot be said too often that very great care must be taken in the use of electricity in laundry. This is because:

(*a*) Water is likely to be about everywhere
(*b*) Some laundry appliances have moving parts.

General rules are:

1. All laundry equipment **must** be properly EARTHED. 3-pin plug tops and socket outlets must be used and fitted properly.
2. At the least sign of any fault, don't use the appliance—get it checked and repaired as soon as possible by a qualified electrician.
3. Make sure you really know how to use and care for your appliances, home demonstrations are best. Read the directions several times too. Hang them near the equipment if possible.
4. Be extra careful with flexes.
5. Put everything away properly after use. (Plugs out.)
6. It's safer **not** to let small children "help".

Washing machines

(*a*) Don't put too many clothes in as this may put too much work on the motor.
(*b*) Remember to dry your hands before touching the switches.
(*c*) Reminder—loose clothes, long chains, necklaces, long hair, can all get caught in washing machines and cause very serious accidents.
(*d*) NEVER put things in or take things out whilst the washing machine or spin drier is working.

Irons

(*a*) Never stand on a wet floor to iron.
(*b*) Don't use the iron if it tingles even a little bit when you touch it.
(*c*) Keep the hand dry which touches the iron.
(*d*) A safety stand prevents dropping accidents.
(*e*) Reminder—never use an iron from a light or lamp socket. Use a 3-pin plug top and socket outlet properly connected.
(*f*) Never use an iron if the cover is cracked.

WET—
DANGER !

GENERAL NOTES

(*a*) Put the iron in a safe place to cool off, not on the ironing board.
(*b*) Don't wrap the flex round a hot iron.
(*c*) Don't keep banging it down when using.
(*d*) Unplug it after use.

Floors

Extra safety notes are:

(*a*) Concrete, stone or tiled floors—when these get wet the danger of being killed by an electric shock is greater still. 3-pin plug tops and socket outlets properly connected are a must on all electrical appliances.
(*b*) Even if the floor is not usually slippery, water, soap, and some detergents may make it very slippery.

Drying and airing (see also pp. 242–3)

Extra safety notes are:

(*a*) Clothes horses and airers must be stable.

(b) Airers which can be pulled up to the ceiling do fall down sometimes. Make sure they are very secure.

(c) Make sure all airers work easily and save pinched fingers.

(d) Many housewives sprain ankles whilst hanging out the clothes. Make sure there is a good safe path or level ground where the clothes line is.

(e) Only one person at a time should use a wringer. Keep small children right away.

SEWING SAFELY

Sewing accidents are usually of the following kinds, and most of them can be avoided:

Cuts from scissors and razor blades
Pins and needles sticking in people
Pins being swallowed
Machine accidents.

Scissors and razor blades

(a) Sharp scissors are safer than blunt ones, but keep them out of children's way.

(b) Keep razor blades in a little tin and put them in it when finished with. Keep the tin in a safe place.

Pins and needles

(a) Don't put pins in the mouth.

(b) Don't stick pins or needles in dress fronts, chairs, or any other place where they may stick in people.

(c) Do be extra careful when mending mattresses, pillows, bed linen and cushions, not to leave the needle or pins in.

(d) Be extra careful with very large needles, e.g. packing needles. Keep them in a safe place.

(e) Keep sewing baskets and boxes away from small children. Most things in them are dangerous to little ones. Boxes could be locked.

(f) Thimbles can prevent very bad fingers.

(g) Use a big magnet to pick pins up from the floor.

(h) Shield needles with the hand when hand sewing. Children and pets can easily be hurt otherwise.

Machines

(a) Electric—Keep all the safety rules for using electricity.

(*b*) Hand—It is always dangerous for one person to do the sewing whilst another person turns the handle.

(*c*) Treadle—Keep a watch for small children and pets under the machine.

(*d*) When using any kind of machine, take reasonable care to keep your fingers, and children's fingers, away from the needle.

Safer not to have children around when using machines, but not always possible of course.

(*e*) A light on the machine helps to prevent accidents.

(*f*) If there are children about, machines and machine drawers should be kept locked when not being used.

(*g*) Don't leave machine oil around. A child may drink it. Lock it up when finished with.

Shield the needle with your hand when sewing

PETS

Pets themselves and, most important, the family and others, will be a lot safer if:

1. Pets are kept under control

2. They are taught safety rules
3. They are kept clean and healthy.

INDOORS

They can cause fires by
tossing paper about
knocking over oil stoves
chewing flexes.

They can cause falls by
sitting on stairs
getting under foot.

To prevent such accidents pets must be housetrained for safety. It takes time but can save lives. Training centres are a great help.

OUTDOORS

1. Dogs should be kept on a short lead in busy streets.
2. Teach them "kerb drill" and save motoring accidents.
3. Teach them not to foul the pavement and save people falling.
4. Teach them not to jump up; big dogs can knock children or elderly people over doing this.
5. Keep them tethered when in cars for safety.
6. Try not to take them into food shops.
7. Never exercise them whilst riding a bicycle.

HEALTH

For the health of the family animals should be kept as clean and healthy as possible.

It is safer if they have their own dishes and a separate knife and fork is used for preparing their food. Wash these things separately too. Make sure they have their own piece of towel also.

Never put a puppy's or kitten's training box in the kitchen where food is prepared. Get them trained to go out as soon as possible.

Be very careful if there are small children in the house who will "eat anything". They must not touch the animal's training box, or

(*a*) take the animal to bed
(*b*) eat after playing with the animal. Wash the child's hands first.

Make sure a puppy has been properly wormed before you bring it into a home with small children. Best to take it to a veterinary surgeon who will check it when necessary. Children can become very ill if worm eggs are able to get into their mouths and are eaten.

HANDYMAN AND REPAIRS

A good handyman (man or woman) in the home can be a real life-saver.

But

Many deaths and serious injuries are caused every year by "do it yourself" people.

Before attempting any household job which could cause an accident if badly done, the handyman should ask himself:

(*a*) Do I really understand what needs to be done?
(*b*) Have I the **knowledge** to do it?
(*c*) Have I the **skill** to do it SAFELY?

Knowledge can be obtained from:
Evening classes
Correspondence courses
Books

Skill comes from:
Practice
Ability.

All first attempts at jobs where safety is important should be:

(*a*) Done under supervision
(*b*) Checked for safety by an expert before the thing is put into use.

It is important to know **when to call the expert,** e.g. **call him:**

When you are not quite sure what is wrong.
If you are not certain how to do it.
If you've never done it before.
For all gas repairs.
For electric repairs apart from mending fuses and connecting plug tops.
If there's likely to be any danger in doing the job.
If there's likely to be any danger if the job is not done correctly.
If you are at all nervous about doing the job.

Before attempting any jobs to do with the structure of the home:

You must KNOW YOUR HOUSE, e.g.

What the parts are made of
Where gas pipes, electric cables and water pipes run.
Danger points—where not to stand in the loft, etc.

Equipment

Proper equipment is best. Make-do equipment must be safe.
Ladders and steps must be strong and non-slip.
Scaffolding—best to borrow the real thing.
Proper lights—lamps on flexes are never safe.
Use proper inspection lamps, fully insulated and guarded.
Lifting equipment—safer to borrow some rather than have an accident.

Tools

Make sure you know **any risks** involved in using them.
Make sure you know **how** to use them.
Use the right tools for the job.
Look after tools properly.
Where possible buy safety tools (the best are usually safest) e.g.

Insulated screwdrivers, etc. for electrical jobs.
Rubber-covered torch
Hammers and choppers with heads that won't fly off.

The greatest care must be taken in choosing and using electrical tools. Safer if they are run from a battery or their own transformer than from the main supply, if they are likely to be used outdoors.

PROPER EVERYTHING is the number one must. The tool which is safe on a dry job might kill you if you use it in the presence of water.

Materials

For safety's sake you must know something of the properties of the materials used, e.g.

Is it inflammable?
Is it poisonous?
Is there any risk of explosion?
Is it dangerous if breathed in?
    etc.

If the container doesn't tell you, ASK the shopkeeper or write to the manufacturer.

Spares

Make sure you keep spares for anything which:

(*a*) May cause an accident if you haven't a spare
(*b*) May cause an accident if you have to use something else to "make do".

General care

All equipment, tools and materials must be:

(a) Used with care
(b) Put away after use
(c) Stored carefully and safely
(d) Kept away from children if:

> Likely to be dangerous in any way
> Likely to cause an accident in an emergency if mislaid.

Protection

Overalls are safer than loose jackets, etc.
Goggles—must be worn where there is any danger of dust, etc. getting into the eyes.
Helmets—to protect from falls or falling articles.
Masks—are a safety must if a long job is being done where dust or fumes are likely to be breathed in.
Gloves—should be worn when safer.
Safety harness or strap when working in high places.
Women handymen need to dress for the job too, e.g.

> "High heels and ladders" are dangerous
> Slacks are safer than skirts.
> Long hair is dangerous if machinery is being used.
> Dressing for the job is never "cissy". Not dressing for the job is always stupid.

Some do's and don'ts

1. Don't put plug sockets in bathrooms.
2. Don't put long flexes on electric kettles.
3. Don't use blow lamps to thaw frozen pipes.
4. Don't go higher than you feel safe.
5. Don't bang nails in walls unless you are sure gas pipes, electric cables, etc. are nowhere about.
6. Do fix ladders securely. Fasten tall ladders at the top.
7. Do switch off electricity at the mains before doing any electrical job, even changing lamps.
8. Do work in a good light.
9. Do clean yourself up properly after doing jobs.
10. Do test jobs for safety before leaving them or putting a repaired article back into use.
11. Do make sure the workshop is safe in every way, is kept tidy and locked if small children are about.
12. DO CALL IN EXPERTS BEFORE IT'S TOO LATE.

REPAIRS

Any repair which involves SAFETY should be done as soon as possible. Keep a look out for these:

Inside the house

1. Broken stairs and banisters.
2. Broken or loose floor boards.
3. Worn floor covering and stair coverings.
4. Windows—broken sash cords, loose fastenings, sticking, cracked or broken glass.
5. Ceilings—check any cracks.
6. Open fires—broken fire backs and hearths.
7. Any electric, gas and oil appliances not working properly.
8. Dry rot.

Outside the house

1. Loose tiles.
2. Loose, rusty or broken pipes and gutterings. (Paint for safety too.)
3. Broken or loose chimneys and chimney stacks.
4. Any flue outlets which have become stopped up.
5. Broken paths or steps.
6. Broken fences or gates (especially where there are children).

Get rid of

All broken things which cannot be mended, especially china and glass or anything else which may be at all dangerous.

Gas

The main gas accidents are:

Poisoning
Explosion
Fires

To prevent accidents in the use of gas it is necessary to know:

(*a*) When gas can be dangerous
(*b*) Something about how the installations and appliances work
(*c*) How to use and care for the installations and appliances.

GENERAL CARE

1. Report any leak to the Gas Board **at once**. Turn off the gas at the main switch first if you can. Open the window.

    If gas smells strong when you enter the house:

    (*a*) Don't switch electric switches on. Even this can cause an explosion.

    (*b*) Don't go in. (Go and 'phone the Gas Board's emergency number.)

2. NEVER look for a gas leak with a naked light, e.g.

    Matches
    Candles
    Lighters
    Lighted paper.

3. Only qualified gas fitters should do the following jobs. It is not safe for anybody else to attempt them.

    Installing gas pipes and appliances
    Repairs
    Special cleaning and overhauling (a yearly check-up of all equipment is advisable).

4. Somebody in the house should be responsible for checking all appliances every so often to make sure they are working properly.

5. Make sure that anybody who is likely to use an appliance knows how to use it properly. (This includes guests.)

6. It is not safe to use appliances for the wrong purposes, e.g. drying clothes over cookers.

7. All large equipment must be properly vented by flues or air bricks so that fumes can be taken outside the house.

    When using small appliances without flues, it is always safer to make sure there is some ventilation, e.g. the window open just a little. Hearth type fires must be properly fitted into a fireplace with an open chimney.

8. All tubing should be the metal type. This applies to ends of tubes and gas connections too.

9. All old-fashioned equipment and appliances should be replaced with modern safe ones, but this can be quite dear to do.

10. Take extra care:

    If anybody in the house can't smell properly. (Test everybody to make sure.)

If anybody is likely to turn taps on. Very old people do this
as well as children sometimes for no apparent reason.
If very depressed people live in the house.

11. Always make sure:

Gas appliances are properly alight when you light them.
Gas taps are really off when you have finished using the
appliance.

12. If **any** gas taps are loose or can be knocked on or off by
furniture near them, when you walk past them, or by children,
have safety taps fitted or put the appliance in a better place.

13. If gas is turned off at the mains for any reason, make sure all
gas taps and pilot lights are turned off too, or gas will escape
when the main is turned on again.

DANGER!

WARNING SIGNS

Don't ignore any of these signs. If you do there may be an
explosion, or a fire, or somebody may get poisoned and die!

1. Smell of gas when no burner is alight
2. Burners, etc. which won't light properly
3. Whistling

4. Repeated "popping"
5. Loose connections
6. Stiff or loose taps
7. Cracked pipes
8. If people continually feel drowsy or headachey in a room where a gas appliance is being used, but feel all right elsewhere.

DANGER LIST

1. Hard bangs on pipes, connectors, appliances, etc.
2. Using very old appliances.
3. Using very old equipment.
4. Turning on gas before striking match, etc.

Light the match BEFORE you turn on the tap

5. Leaving fires or gas rings at low all night or when you are out.
6. Cooking boiling over and putting out gas whilst you are not in the room.
7. Leaving taps turned on when shilling has run out whilst you put another one in.
8. Sharing a meter with other tenants.

9. Not knowing how to turn the gas off at the main or not being able to because it is too stiff.
10. Draughts which cause pilot lights, gas rings, etc. to blow out.
11. Faulty flues, stopped-up vents.
12. Gas points no longer used which have not been sealed off.
13. Throwing matches etc. into the radiants of gas fires.

Extra notes

Cookers

1. Always make sure that all gas taps are off except for those you are using (especially oven).
2. Be extra careful if the Regulo and gas are controlled by the same tap.
3. If a gas blows out while you are in the room, turn the tap off and wait a minute or two before lighting it again.
4. If a lot of gas has escaped, turn off taps and open windows wide to let gas out. Don't relight until all smell has gone.
5. Make sure there are no draughts while you are cooking.
6. Don't use the oven for heating the room for long periods. (Have the window open a little too.)
7. Make sure pilot light doesn't go out if the cooker has automatic lighting.
8. Make sure all the taps are off when you go out or when you go to bed at night.

Water heaters

1. Make sure there is no draught strong enough to blow out pilot light.
2. Always turn off water heater before getting into a bath.
3. Always have the window open a little while the heater is on.
4. Make sure the flue is kept clear.

Fires

1. Flat top fires—don't air clothes on the top. Never put papers on the top.
2. Always make sure that all the burners are alight.
3. If any radiants are broken, get them replaced quickly.
4. Don't let fluff, dust or other rubbish collect behind or underneath fires.
5. Don't put portable fires where they can set fire to beds, other furniture or curtains.
6. Make sure they stand firm on something that won't burn, e.g. a tin tray.

Electricity

The main electrical accidents which can happen are:

Electrocution and burns
Fire

To prevent accidents in the use of electricity it is necessary to know:

(*a*) When electricity can be dangerous
(*b*) Something about how the installation and appliances work
(*c*) How to use and care for the general installation and for appliances.

GENERAL CARE

1. Ideally installations should be checked every five years.
2. All repairs and additional wiring should be done by a qualified electrician.
   Mending fuses and connecting plug tops can be done at home, but even these jobs can cause fatal accidents if not done correctly.
3. All fixed appliances should be fitted by a qualified electrician.
4. Anybody using an appliance must know how to use it correctly.
5. All appliances must be used for the correct purposes, e.g. turning electric fires on to their backs and cooking on them is dangerous.
6. Somebody should be responsible for checking all appliance flexes etc. about every three months, especially before winter.
   Large equipment and equipment often used should be checked from time to time by a qualified electrician.
7. Make sure the installation is correctly earthed.

WARNING SIGNS

If any of the following are ignored, fire might break out or somebody may be electrocuted.

1. Burning smell from hot cables
2. Flashes
3. Crackling sounds
4. Fuses keep blowing

5. Plugs, sockets, or switches feeling warm
6. Plugs, sockets, or switches which are broken, cracked or loose
7. Flickering lights
8. Flexes frayed or damaged in any way.

Note

Never leave repairs "till later", somebody might use the appliance. Warn everybody in case.

ELECTRICITY AND WATER—specially dangerous

Electricity passes through water easily. If a person whose body is touching water, or is wet with perspiration, touches a live wire or a faulty appliance, they are more likely to be electrocuted.

DANGER LIST

1. Putting hot water bottles in beds when an electric blanket is being used.
2. Using electric blankets if the person is likely to wet the bed, e.g. children, sick people, very old people. (Check with makers.)
3. Standing on a wet floor when ironing, or ironing with wet hands.
4. Putting fires on a wet floor.
5. Putting fires in bathrooms (except specially installed wall fires—and don't let these be fixed over the bath).
6. Touching any electric appliance that has fallen into water without switching off the electricity and pulling the plug out, e.g. shavers, toothbrushes, etc.
7. Standing vases of flowers on radios, televisions, electric heaters, etc.
8. Washing hand electric mixers under the tap while still plugged in, even if switched off. (Take beaters out to wash them.)
9. Filling or pouring from kettles or percolators whilst they are plugged in, even if switched off.
10. Cleaning a cooker before it is switched off.
11. Washing sockets, switches or light bulbs when electricity is not switched off by the main switch.
12. Taking things out of the wash boiler when the plug is not out.
13. Touching switches, plugs, appliances, etc., with wet hands.
14. Taking radios, hairdryers, etc., in to bathrooms.

Don't take this in, it could kill you

Extra notes

Reasonable care must be taken in the use of anything to do with electricity.

1. Don't knock switches, sockets, etc., whilst working.
2. Don't let plugs drop on floor, bang against walls, etc.
3. Never treat anything electrical roughly, e.g. banging it down, banging into it.
4. Use 3-pin plugs properly earthed on all appliances except those which are double insulated.

Extra Do's and Don'ts

1. Toasters—If bread gets stuck in the toaster, take out plug before poking bread out.

2. Kettles—Don't let the kettle flex trail over the stove, it will get charred and fray.

Never let anybody put a longer flex on it so that you can fill it while it's plugged in.

3. Electric blankets

Use them according to instructions.

Store carefully in summer.

Have them checked before winter. (Don't leave unchecked for more than three years.)

Don't leave them on all the time, e.g. when you go away at the weekend, to keep the bed aired.

4. Irons—Take care not to drop them, keep banging them down, or let them get knocked over. Always switch them off and take plug out if you have to leave the room. Use a proper iron-stand.

5. Fans—Make sure flex or anything else is not touching blades. Blades must be quite free before switching on.

6. Fires

Never touch an element when the plug is not out.

Don't air clothes on convector heaters.

For other fire risks, see section on Fire.

7. Lights and lamps—Don't leave light or lamp holders without bulbs in them.

Never touch the place where the bulb goes in, unless the main switch is off.

It's always safer to turn the main switch off before changing bulbs. Any metal switches should be got rid of as soon as possible.

Light switches should be just inside the door.

Bathrooms should only have cord switches. Some people prefer to have the switch outside the door.

8. Cookers, washing machines, drying machines, washing up machines—If they show the smallest sign of not working properly, don't use them.

Call a qualified electrician, do not attempt to repair them yourself.

It is essential that they are all earthed.

9. Never disconnect a flex at the appliance and leave the plug hanging in the socket, whether it is switched off or not.

10. Always switch electricity off at the socket and pull out plugs of all-appliances when not being used. This should be somebody's job before going to bed. (Fridges, water heaters, central heating may be left on.)

11. If you use a faulty electric appliance and touch a water pipe at the same time, you could be electrocuted.

12. Don't leave things which can be set on fire in front of a fire which is operated by a time switch and set to go on whilst you are out.

Special note

Try not to have small children around when:

(*a*) Electricians are doing repairs

(*b*) Television and radio repairers are working.

Qualified electricians often **appear** to take risks. Small children may easily copy (and not so small children too).

PLUGS AND SOCKETS

It is important always to use 3-pin plugs and sockets for safety. This is because one of the pins is an **earthing** pin (the long one).

When the appliance is plugged in, the earthing pin goes into a hole in the socket which is connected to the **earth.**

If the appliance or connection is faulty the electric current will pass into the earth instead of into the person.

As well as using 3-pin plugs and sockets it is also important

(*a*) To use the correct fuse.

(*b*) To connect the flex properly to the plug. If you are not certain how to do this get a qualified electrician to do it.

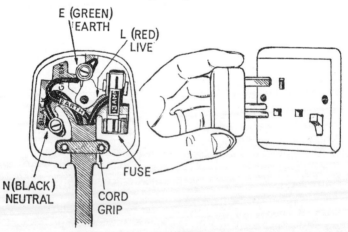

Universal (13 amp) switched socket outlet and standard plug with built-in fuse

Notes

1. If you buy an appliance which has not been made in Britain, take it to an electrician to check which of the wires is which, e.g. the earth wire may be red instead of green.
2. Some appliances are made safe by being double insulated e.g. some hair driers. In this case you don't need to use the earth pin in the plug top. It may be safer to check with the Electricity Board before using the appliance.
3. Modern 13-amp plugs are the most useful.

   (a) They have safety shutters.
   (b) They can be used for any appliance up to 3,000 watts (with the correct fuse in).
   (c) They carry their own fuse, a cartridge fuse, easy to renew.

Reminders

1. Wrong connections can cause somebody to be killed.
2. Sockets must never be put in bathrooms or too near sinks in kitchens (exception—a properly fitted shaving socket in the bathroom, out of reach of the person in the bath).
3. Sockets should be placed near to where the appliance is to be used to prevent trailing wires.

   Put them at the most convenient height for working and a safe height where there are small children.
4. Sockets are safer still if they have their own switches.

FUSES

The safety points to remember about fuses are:

1. Don't try to mend or replace them unless you really know how to.
2. Remember a fuse is **meant** to be a weak spot so that it will "blow" when anything is wrong and so prevent an accident.

   This means it is very dangerous to use a fuse wire or a cartridge fuse too large for the appliance. Always use the correct size.

Note

   13-amp plugs are sold with 13-amp fuse cartridges in them. If you only need a 3-amp fuse you must buy it as well as the plug. It is a good idea to keep a few spares of both sizes in the house.
3. Never use anything but proper fuse wire for a wired fuse.

4. If you keep getting blown fuses it's safer to consult a qualified electrician.

5 Never touch the Electricity Board Fuse Box.

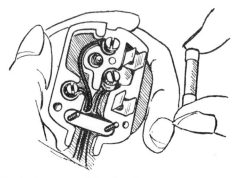

Replacing a cartridge fuse in a 13-amp plug top

Recommended Fuse Sizes for 13-amp Plug tops
3 amp (Blue)

Radio	Percolators
Television	Food mixers
Lamps (table, standard, portable)	Refrigerators
Shavers	Hair driers
Fans	Vacuum cleaners
Electric blankets	Unheated washing machines
	Spin driers

plus all other appliances up to 720 watts.

13 amp (Brown)

1, 2 and 3 bar fires	Tumbler driers
Convector heaters	Irons
Fan heaters	Toasters
Drying cabinets	Heated washing machines
Immersion heaters	Kettles
	Water heaters

plus all other appliances from 720 watts up to 3,000 watts.

Notes

1. 3,000 watts is often called 3 kW.

2. Look on the nameplate of the appliance for information too.
3. Check with local Electricity Board if not quite sure.

FLEX

The fact that electricity runs through flex is not always sufficiently realised, especially by children. It should be constantly checked and always used carefully.

Frayed flex = DANGER

Here are some points to watch:

1. Don't use flex which is longer than necessary.
2. A long flex should be run along the wall. Fix it with insulated hooks, never with metal staples, or over nails, etc.
3. Don't run flex under mats or carpets or lino. In time the flex will fray and start a fire.
4. Check flex often for fraying, especially where it joins the plug or appliance.
5. Never pin Christmas decorations on flex and never hang anything on flex.
6. Try not to let flex trail around for people to trip over it.
7. It is better **never** to repair flex but to have new flex fitted. If you do repair it in an emergency, be sure to use insulating tape and get new flex fitted as soon as possible. (Don't forget to switch electricity off at the mains first.)

8. Don't connect new flex to an appliance yourself. Take it to an electrician.
9. Never tug at the flex to pull out a plug.
10. Never use flex all twisted up and don't roll it up too tightly.
11. Use correct size flex—good electrical shops will advise.
12. Don't tie knots in flexes. Have them the right length or use correct clips.

OVERLOADING

Overloading means making the wires carry too much current. This happens when:

1. Power appliances are run from the light circuit.
2. Too many appliances are run from one power point.
3. Too many appliances are run at the same time for the house's electric installation.

If lighting or power circuits are overloaded the wires get too hot and might cause a fire.

Remember the wires may be under the floor boards or embedded in the walls, which may mean a fire has got a good hold before it is discovered.

To prevent overloading:

1. Don't run fires, irons, toasters, vacuum cleaners, etc. from light holders.
2. Make sure you have enough power points or sockets.
3. Get an electrician to tell you the total load your electric installation can carry. It's safer than trying to work it out for yourself.
4. Twin sockets are better than adaptors.

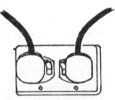

Twin sockets help to avoid overloading

Gardens

Gardens should be places of happiness and relaxation, but they are often the place of accident and even death.

By taking extra care in the following ways, gardens can be made much safer.

Tidiness

1. Keep the garden clear of dangerous rubbish—

   Broken glass and plant pots
   Bits of wood
   Bits of wire
   Rusty nails

2. Make sure toys and tools are put away after use.

   (a) They can be tripped over
   (b) Children can get badly hurt playing with dangerous tools.

3. There must be safe storage space for:

   All garden sprays, etc.
   Large and small tools.
   Fuel oils.

4. Milk bottles—either make sure small children can't get at them or keep them indoors until the milkman calls.

Garden jobs

All jobs which make the garden safer must be kept up to date, e.g.

1. Keep paths and steps in good repair.
2. Do repairs to fences and gates.
3. Long grass can hide dangerous objects—short grass is safer. Very small children can get hurt if they can't be seen.
4. Keep used paths clear of snow and ice in winter.

Using equipment

1. All equipment must be used with care.
2. Small children must never be allowed to use tools, etc., which could hurt them.
3. Older children must be properly taught how to use forks, mowers, etc.

4. All electrical equipment must be earthed and used with special care, e.g.

Power mowers—be careful small children don't get in the way, Hedge clippers—take care not to cut the flex.

5. Keep all equipment in good repair, especially power and cutting tools.

Garages

1. Should never be used as playrooms—separate sheds are better, however small.
2. It's safer not to use them as rubbish dumps or storerooms.
3. Oil stoves and electric fires should not be used in garages.
4. Only lights properly fixed by a qualified electrician are safe.
5. New buildings must be passed and inspected by the Local Authority.

   Old garages should be properly ventilated and made fireproof.

Sheds

1. If they contain any dangerous tools or poisonous substances. they must be kept locked and out of bounds for children.
2. Children's play sheds should be:

   (*a*) As fireproof as possible
   (*b*) Properly ventilated
   (*c*) Inspected by parents every now and again for safety's sake!

Greenhouses, etc.

1. Greenhouses, cold frames etc. must be kept out of bounds for small children.
2. Cracked or broken glass must be quickly replaced or properly removed.
3. Fertiliser etc.—If they must be kept in the greenhouse the door must be kept locked.

Water (see also p. 96)

Swimming pools

(*a*) Rules regarding use must be made and kept.
(*b*) A really safe cover is vital if there are small children.
(*c*) A life-line rope is a must.
(*d*) Lighting must be fixed by a qualified electrician.

Even the shallowest ornamental pond can be dangerous to a child of "crawling" age.

For extra safety

1. Properly fixed lights by steps, water and any other dangerous spot.
2. Prevent falls by:

    (a) Using non-slip paving stones for paths and steps.
    (b) Keeping paths clear of wet leaves, mud, snails' trails, etc.
    (c) Keeping paths clear of oil, petrol, etc.
    (d) Fixing hand rails on steps.

3. NEVER leave a small child in the garden when cars are coming in or out. Check small children's whereabouts **before** driving in or out.
4. Check all plants and trees to see if they are poisonous.

    (a) Get help from experienced gardeners
    (b) Write to Kew Gardens, London, for advice

5. Chop down any trees which may be dangerous. It's safer to get a big tree cut down by experts.
6. Don't let small children come near when you are doing dangerous jobs.
7. Gates—make sure bars are close enough to prevent children crawling through and fasteners are child proof.

Children

Falls

Falls are the cause of many small children being killed or badly hurt. Once toddlers start walking and climbing the danger of falling becomes greater.

SOME WAYS CHILDREN FALL

1. Down stairs
2. Out of windows
3. Off balconies
4. Off tables, chairs and other furniture
5. Out of prams, cots, and high chairs
6. By slipping

    (*a*) on wet, greasy or shiny floors
    (*b*) in the bath

7. By tripping over things on the floor
8. By tripping over because their shoes are not on properly or don't fit.

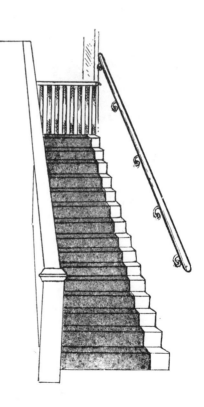

HOW TO PREVENT DANGEROUS FALLS

The main rules are:

Careful watching
Making things as safe as possible

1. Stairs

(a) A gate at top and bottom is safest.

A gate at the top of the stairs must not open towards the stairs.

Gates must have the kind of fastener that small children can't open.

Some safety gates can be fixed to doors too.

(b) Things must not be left on the stairs.

(c) Coverings and stair rods must be firmly fixed and in good repair.

(d) An extra banister at child height means extra safety even if it is only made of rope.

(e) Small children should not be allowed to play on the stairs.

(f) Repair any loose banisters as quickly as possible.

2. Windows

(a) Vertical bars are safest in children's rooms. Safer still if they can be removed by adults in case of fire.

(b) Windows should not be left open in such a way that a child could fall out.

(c) Catches should be high enough or of a type that toddlers can't open.

If a window needs to be left open a little way it should fasten firmly in that position.

3. Balconies

(a) Should be boarded in to a height of four feet.

(b) Stools, boxes or anything a child can stand on should not be left on the balcony.

(c) Small children should never be left alone on high balconies.

4. Tables, chairs and other furniture

(a) Never leave a small baby alone on a table or chair even for one minute.

(b) Don't leave toddlers sitting on a table while you go to fetch something.

(c) Children love climbing over furniture; if the furniture is easy to tip over the child will need extra watching!

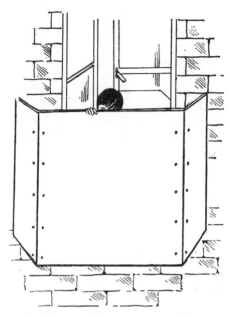

Safe balcony for an upstairs window

5. Prams, cots and high chairs

(*a*) Safety straps are a must to prevent children from falling out of prams and high chairs. Check the "anchor points" of these.

(*b*) Prams should not tip up.

Brakes should be fixed to at least two wheels.

It should not be possible for the pram to run away when the brake is on.

(*c*) Wire trays under the pram for shopping are safer than heavy shopping at one end that can help tip a pram over.

(*d*) Riding seats for toddlers must be properly fixed or the pram will tip over.

(*e*) Check clips if pram is collapsible.

(*f*) Look for the KITE mark.

(*g*) Cots should have safe fastenings so that a child cannot lower the drop side.

(*h*) The sides and ends of the cot should be at least 24 inches high from the wire mattress, 19 inches high from a spring mattress.

Bars should not allow a child's head through

(*i*) The bars must not be more than 3 inches apart.
(*j*) The cot must stand firm and be strongly made.
(*k*) It must be painted or lacquered with non-poisonous paints, etc. (Be very careful with secondhand cots or when painting them yourself. Look for B.S. number when buying paint.)

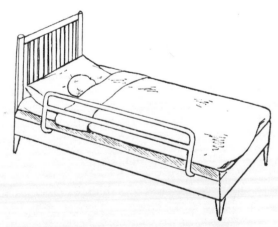

A safe type of cot (the unguarded side goes against the wall)

6. Wet, greasy or shiny floors

Toddlers are not very firm on their feet, so that even a little slip may mean a nasty fall.

- (*a*) Wipe up spills at once.
- (*b*) No polish is better than a slippery floor.
- (*c*) Either don't have small mats or make sure they won't slip, e.g. buy non-slip ones, or nail them down firmly.

7. Baths and toilets

- (*a*) A non-slip mat in the bottom of the bath will help keep a child steady.
- (*b*) A safety rail for a child to hang on to helps too by baths and lavatories.
- (*c*) A "fence" fitted in the bath to make it shorter when a child is being bathed is safer, or use a child's bath seat.
- (*d*) Fix a long "chain" in the lavatory if it has that sort. It saves children standing on the lavatory seat to reach the chain.

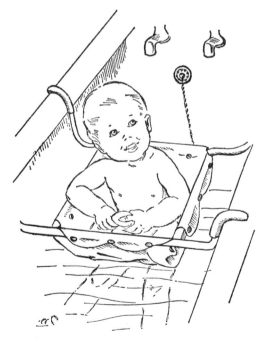

Safety for the child who has outgrown his baby bath

8. Tripping over things

(a) Fringes on mats or worn places will trip a child and make him fall.

(b) It is safest to try to keep the floor clear of things he may trip over, but it's not always possible.

9. Shoes and other clothes

(a) Shoes undone or on the wrong feet can cause a child to fall.

(b) Badly fitting shoes can cause falls too.

(c) Trousers hanging down can trip any child. Trousers with shoulder straps are less likely to fall down.

 # Cuts, Scratches, etc.

Anything pointed or with a sharp edge is dangerous to small children.

They can be badly cut or scratched by anything with a sharp edge.

Pointed things may scratch them or stick into them and may even kill them.

Here are some of the things which should always be kept away from little children:

Opened tins
Broken glass, china, etc.
Sewing things which are sharp or pointed
Tools which are sharp or pointed
Jewellery with sharp points or stones
Knives
Razor blades
Compasses, pens, etc.

Tins

The kind that have to be opened with a tin opener must be thrown away at once.

Never give this kind to children to put their things in.

Never give a child any tin if the edge is sharp.

Broken things

All broken things which have a sharp edge must be thrown away at once, e.g. glass, china, some plastics, some toys.

This means checking children's toys every now and again and removing dangerous ones tactfully.

See p. 116.

Sewing things

e.g. Scissors, pins, needles, must not be kept where a child can get them.

As well as this, try to:

(*a*) Keep the needle point under your hand when you sew. It's quite easy.
(*b*) Remember not to stick pins and needles in the front of your dress or jacket.
(*b*) Keep safety pins closed.

See also p. 51.

Tools

Children reach up and grab the blades of saws, choppers, etc., in a second. Either don't have the child around when jobs are being done or be very careful to keep cutting tools away from the child.

Remember to keep all pointed tools away from children too. This means nails and screws as well.

Jewellery

If at any time you are likely to hold a small baby or play with a toddler, remember these things can scratch or stick in the child and hurt it badly.

Brooches—the pin or any sharp edges
Rings—sharp edged stones
Any jewellery—with sharp points or edges

It is never safe to put brooches, however small, on to babies' clothes.

Knives

Children love cutting things and will get hold of knives whenever they can. It is important to:

(*a*) Keep all knives in a place where small children can't get them. Table drawers are not always the safest place.
(*b*) When the table is being set don't put knives (or forks either) near the edge of the table.

(c) When knives are being used for cooking try to remember not to leave them on the edge of the table.

(d) It is not safe to show small children how to open pen knives.

See also p. 45.

Razor blades

These are terribly dangerous to little children. Great care must be taken to keep them in a safe place.

(a) In the bathroom:

Put used ones in a tin with a lid
Keep new and old ones where children can't reach them.

(b) Train older children to keep any blades they use for hobbies in a tin and not to leave them where small children can get them.

China and glass

Very small children should never be given china or glass things to carry, although they love to bring in a bottle of milk, etc. If they fall over whilst carrying things made of china or glass, they are likely not only to drop, say the bottle, but also to fall onto the broken pieces and get cut badly.

Compasses, etc.

Older children must be told to keep such things as compasses, pens, etc., away from their small brothers and sisters.

Any sharp instrument or toy which older children may be able to use without hurting themselves must be kept away from the small ones. This is always difficult because little children love to join in.

"Cutting out"

At a certain stage children enjoy cutting shapes out of paper or card, and this is a valuable part of their education, but while they are beginners they should be given short-bladed scissors with rounded ends. This could even be an economy if it saves your dressmaking scissors from ruin!

Notes

Keep floors well swept especially if the child is crawling. All sorts of sharp things can stick into them otherwise, e.g. nails, odd staples, drawing pins, etc.

If a child has to wear glasses, it is best to have them fitted with safety lenses if possible.

Electrocution

If an electric current goes through a person's body and into the earth the person is ELECTROCUTED.

Grown-ups can often be saved in time but little children often get killed if they are electrocuted.

Some of the things which can electrocute small children are:

1. Open power points
2. Table lamps
3. Flexes
4. Electric blankets
5. Televisions and radios
6. Any other electrical appliances

1. Power points

If a child sticks a thin metal object into the little holes, the child can be electrocuted.

The kind of things children stick in the little holes are long nails, metal skewers, steel knitting needles, bits of toys, etc.

To make power points safe it is important to:

(*a*) Use **safety** power points. The new 13-amp socket outlets are safe. These have a little shutter behind the pin holes so that metal objects can't be pushed in when there is no plug in.

(*b*) If you can't have safety power points, buy some dummy plugs to put in the power point when the power point is not being used.

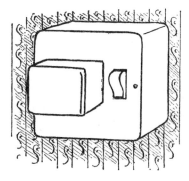

Dummy plug for safety

(c) If you can't manage to get safety power points or dummy plugs make sure that there is a piece of furniture or something in front of each power point to stop a small child getting to it. This is not safe if the child can move it, of course.

(d) If the power points can be put higher up the wall it will be safer for very small children.

2. Table lamps

If there is no bulb in the table lamp, children can push their fingers or metal objects in the hole where the bulb goes.

It is safer to:

(a) Never leave a lamp without a bulb.
(b) If you have to borrow the bulb to use somewhere else, make sure the lamp is not connected to the electricity supply.
(c) If possible, keep table lamps out of the reach of small children, especially in their bedrooms.

3. Flexes

Any flex which is the least bit frayed is likely to be dangerous to small children.

This is because:

(a) Children like picking loose bits off things.
(b) If they grab or crawl on the frayed part they might touch the bare wires.

If possible, little children should not be able to get near any flex at all, because they like chewing things and are even likely to cut a flex if they get the chance.

So it is safer to:

(a) Make sure there are no frayed flexes in use.
(b) Try to keep small children away from all flexes.

4. Electric blankets

Things to think about regarding electric blankets and small children are:

(a) The child must never be allowed to plug it in or out himself. Remember he may get out in the night and do so.
(b) If the child wets the bed he could get electrocuted by some blankets if they were switched on.

5. Televisions and radios

The chief danger with these is that a child can get behind them and stick things in the back! It's safer to:

(a) Put the set where the child can't get behind it. (But not too close to wall or it will overheat.)
(b) Never to leave a little child in a room where he can get behind a television or radio.
(c) Keep your eye on the child.

6. Other electrical appliances

You cannot be too careful about all electrical appliances where small children are. Either don't leave them together or keep constant watch on the child.

See also pp. 62–66.

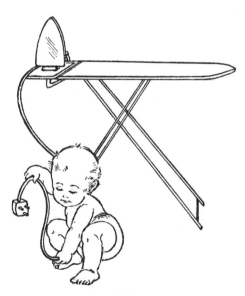

DANGER!

Poisoning

Small children love to do these things:

1. Put things into their mouths
2. Drink out of bottles
3. Eat anything that looks like a sweet.

This means that they can easily eat or drink things that may POISON them.

If children eat POISONOUS things they may:

1. Die
2. Be ill for a very long time.

Nowadays it is harder to keep children safe from poisoning because so many ordinary-looking things used in the home can poison a child.

CHILDREN MAY BE POISONED BY THESE THINGS

1. Medical supplies
2. Perfumes and beauty aids
3. Household cleaners
4. Decorating things
5. Fuel oils
6. Garden sprays, etc.
7. Rat poison, etc.
8. Poisonous plants
9. Gas
10. Alcohol
11. Bad food
    etc.

HOW TO PREVENT CHILDREN BEING POISONED

1. Medical supplies

(a) Medicines which are swallowed.

It must be made IMPOSSIBLE for a small child to get at any of these things:

Bottles of medicine
Tablets
Capsules
Pills
Powders

MEDICINE PILLS SCENT SKIN LOTION IRON PILLS

BLEACH DISINFECTANT FLOOR POLISH SHOE POLISH AMMONIA

TURPENTINE PAINT INSECT SPRAY RAT POISON ALCOHOL

MISTLETOE

Any of these familiar things can be dangerous to a child

These include such things as:

Sleeping pills	Hay fever pills
Aspirins	Nerve pills
Cough mixtures	Heart pills
Vitamin pills	Kidney pills
Iron pills	Sea sickness pills
Slimming tablets	Laxatives
Birth control pills	"Tonics"

(b) Lotions and ointments for external use.
"External use" means for use OUTSIDE the body.
Anything labelled "For external use" must

NEVER BE SWALLOWED.

Even if the tube or bottle does not say "Poison" on it, these kinds of things must be kept away from little children:

Skin creams
Lotions
Eye ointment and drops
Sun tan creams, oils, etc.

Watch that child!

(c) First Aid things—many of these may be poisonous to little children.

(d) Medicine, etc., for animals.

Remember:

(a) A child can swallow in less than a moment.

(b) Even a small child will wait till a grown-up's back is turned to take what it wants.

(c) Toddlers soon learn to climb on chairs to get to medicine and first aid cupboards.

(d) Small children are **very** clever at opening bottles, etc.

(e) Older children love playing nurses and doctors and will dose a little one with real medicine if they get the chance.

See also p. 168.

2. Perfumes and other beauty aids

(a) Little children like the smell and pretty colour of these.

(b) They should not be left where toddlers can get at them, e.g on dressing tables or in drawers that the child can get at.

(c) They will take them out of handbags too.

3. Household cleaners

These include the following:

Bleach
Detergents
Disinfectants
Other cleaning liquids and powders
Polishes
Dry cleaners
Caustic soda.

It is difficult to keep these away from children because they are always being used and need to be handy.

It is best to try not to:

(a) Have children around while you are using them

(b) Leave them where a child can get them whilst they are being used.

When they are not being used they MUST be kept out of children's reach.

They must NEVER be put into soft drink bottles, cups, etc.

See also p. 38.

4. Decorating things

Paints, strippers, turps, etc., are all poison to small children. They should:

(*a*) Be stored where children can't reach them
(*b*) Not be used when toddlers are around
(*c*) Never be put in soft drink bottles.

Paint with lead in it should never be used:

(*a*) Round the house
(*b*) For children's cots, toys, etc.

Children often suck paintwork and get lead poisoning (which may damage their brain).
See also p. 119.

5. Garden sprays, etc.

Many of these will kill a child outright, e.g.

Rat poison
Insect killers
Weed killers
Creosote, etc.

Children must never be allowed to touch them.
See also p. 72.

6. Fuel oils

All these can kill a child and children do drink them.

Paraffin
Petrol and car oil
Methylated spirit.

It must be impossible for a child to drink them.
Be extra careful to keep small bottles of lighter petrol out of a child's reach.

7. Poisonous plants

Here are the names of some plants which can poison children:

Deadly nightshade
Foxglove
Mistletoe
Many fungi (some look like mushrooms)

Many berries, e.g. holly
Rhubarb leaves
Laburnum seeds
Privet

It is safest to get rid of these plants if possible, but it will still be necessary to keep an eye on small children.

Even very young children can be taught not to eat things out of the garden unless they "show Mummy first".

Be careful at Christmas time when holly and mistletoe berries are in the house.

8. Gas poisoning

Never leave a child about in a room if there is a gas tap which can be turned on. Even small babies can do this.

See p. 59 for general gas safety.

9. Alcohol

It is not often realised that a child can be poisoned by drinking alcohol. Care must be taken to see that toddlers don't drink the contents of bottles or glasses.

It is not wise to give small children "little sips"—they are sure to drink more if they get the chance.

A lock-up cupboard is safer for wines, spirits, etc.

10. Bad food

Be extra careful to give small children only fresh food.
See also pp. 110, 182.

Note

1. Many things used in hobbies by the rest of the family can also poison little ones, e.g.

   Liquids used in photography
   Some glues and adhesives
   Inks

2. Children may be poisoned by SMELLING things, e.g.

   Nail polish
   Furniture polish

3. Hungry children are more likely to eat poisonous things, e.g. before mealtimes.

4. It is never safe to give babies or children any medicines unless the doctor says so, and then always give the proper dose.

5. Be very careful which ointments and dusting powders you put on babies, especially if the skin is very sore.
It's safer to ask the doctor about this too.

Scalds

A SCALD is a BURN caused by any very hot liquid (or steam) getting on the skin.
Skin can still be scalded even if:

(a) the water etc. is not boiling but only very hot;
(b) the skin is covered with clothes.

Babies' skins are very tender. Liquid which only feels "quite hot" to adults may scald a baby badly.

HOW DO CHILDREN GET SCALDED?

1. By hot liquid being spilt on them by adults and other children.
2. By pulling hot liquids over themselves.
3. By falling into hot water.
4. By being put into hot water.
5. By eating or drinking food which is too hot.

HOW TO PREVENT CHILDREN BEING SCALDED

There are TWO golden rules.

1. Don't put hot liquids near them.
2. Keep them away from hot liquids.

Neither of these rules is always easy!
Here are some hints:

1. Saucepans and kettles

(a) Never leave pan handles sticking out over the edge of the stove. Children may pull the handle and be scalded by hot liquid coming out of the pan.
(b) Never leave the kettle spout facing the edge of the stove. When it boils, boiling water may fall on the child.

(*c*) Have a saucepan guard fitted to the top of the stove if you can.·

(*d*) Electric kettles—never put them on the floor to boil if there are small children about. Hook the flex up too so that they can't pull it.

2. Food

Don't put their food near them whilst it is hot. Test their drinks before giving them.

3. Tablecloths

Children often pull at a cloth and so pull a teapot of hot tea over themselves. Where there are small children it is best

(*a*) Not to use tablecloths.

(*b*) To make sure the edges don't hang down. One way is to thread elastic through the hem so that the cloth just fits the table top.

(*c*) To take extra care when using a "best" cloth which you want to hang down.

Whether a cloth is used or not, never put the following things near the edge of the table:

Teapots
Hot water jugs
Cups of hot tea, etc.
Jugs of hot gravy, custard, etc.

Note

Be extra careful when using:

Low coffee tables
Trolleys
Trays fixed to chair arms
Ordinary trays.

Some people give up serving hot food and drink on coffee tables, etc. whilst the children are small.

4. Washing and bathing small children

(a) Whether you are using

the big bath
baby's bath
a bowl

ALWAYS put the COLD WATER in FIRST.

(b) Always test the heat of the water **with your elbow** before washing the child.

(c) If possible do not get the water ready when the child is about.
(d) Never leave the child alone with or in the water is a good rule. (It is safer to be around even when older children are bathing.)
(e) Never add hot water to the bath whilst the child is in the bath.

5. Household washing and cleaning

(a) Keep small children away from boilers and washing machines.
(b) Don't leave buckets of hot water around.
(c) Keep an eye on boilers and bowls on stoves. If they boil over a child can be scalded.

See also p. 48.

6. Carrying hot liquids

(a) It's better not to do it if a child is about, but if you must, be very careful.
(b) Never drink hot drinks when nursing a baby.
(c) Never pass hot liquids over a child's head.

7. Hot water bottles for children

(a) Don't use very hot water and never use boiling water.
(b) Make sure the bottles are in good repair.

(*c*) Put a thick cover over them.
(*d*) Put them beneath the under blanket.

Note

This section is about hot liquids scalding small children. It is also very important not to leave a small child alone with boilers and baths, etc. containing warm or cold water. Remember children can be DROWNED in even a FEW INCHES of water.

Suffocation

Suffocation means DYING because you CAN'T BREATHE.
Many children and babies die like this.

HOW DO LITTLE CHILDREN GET SUFFOCATED AND DIE?

1. When these things press on their noses and mouth:

(*a*) Soft pillows, cushions, or mattresses
(*b*) Bed clothes
(*c*) Older people sleeping in the same bed as the children and accidentally lying on them
(*d*) Dogs and cats sitting on them
(*e*) Fold-up cots folding up with the baby inside
(*f*) Things made of plastic
(*g*) Sand
(*h*) Very soft toys.

2. By breathing in these things:

(*a*) Fluff from fluffy materials
(*b*) Fumes from anything smouldering
(*c*) Fumes from gas fires, oil fires, or boilers which are not working properly.
(*d*) Smoke
(*e*) Gas
(*f*) Sickness or mucus.

Baby is safer in his own cot

3. When things get stuck in their throat or windpipe so that they choke and can't breathe:

(a) Eyes from toys, beads, buttons, etc.
(b) Fluff or other bits of material
(c) Dummies
(d) Food and drink (and big sweets).

4. If the inside of the throat swells up because they are ill or get stung.

5. By strangling, e.g. by pram straps, etc.

HOW TO PREVENT children being suffocated

1. Pillows, cushions, mattresses

(a) Firm ones are safest
(b) Small babies don't need a pillow usually
(c) Older babies may have either:

A pillow put under the mattress
A firm pillow
A safety pillow.

2. Plastic

(*a*) Plastic bags—Keep them away from children.

    (i) Small children like to put these on their heads to play spacemen. The plastic sticks on the child's face and can kill it very quickly because it stops the child breathing. The plastic is very hard to remove.

    (ii) Never put children's toys in plastic bags. Take them off new toys.

    (iii) If pillows or mattresses have plastic bags on them, take the bag off as soon as you get home.

(*b*) Pieces or sheets of plastic.

    (i) Don't use plastic sheeting in cots or prams.

    (ii) Don't let children play with pieces or sheets of plastic.

(*c*) Plastic bibs.

    (i) Take the plastic bib off as soon as the baby is fed.

    (ii) Only use them at feeding times.

    (iii) Don't leave the baby alone with a plastic bib on and **never** let him sleep in one.

3. Bedclothes

(*a*) A baby must not be able to slip down so that its head is under the clothes. Tuck him in firmly.

(*b*) Bedclothes must not come up high enough to cover the baby's mouth or nose.

(*c*) Don't cover the baby with anything made of fluffy material in case bits of fluff get into the baby's nose or mouth. Don't put soft fuzzy toys on small babies' pillows.

4. Sleeping

(*a*) Babies should be put to sleep only in a cot or pram.

(*b*) A baby should not sleep with grown-ups or older children in case someone rolls over onto the baby.

(*c*) Cots and prams should be covered with a safety net to keep dogs and cats off.

(*d*) It's best to have a look at a sleeping baby now and again to make sure he's all right.

(e) Fold-up cots must be checked every so often to make sure they won't fold up with the baby inside.

It's safer to only use a cot stand which is made for the cot. Check even these often.

5. Fumes and smoke

(a) If the baby is in a room where clothes are airing, be extra careful not to put the clothes too near the fire.

If the clothes smoulder, the fumes can kill a small baby.

(b) Don't burn material on a fire if a baby is in the room.

(c) Make extra sure that gas fires, oil stoves, and boilers are in perfect working order.

Escaping fumes can kill babies.

(d) Take extra care to see that unlit gas taps are not left on.

(e) Never leave a baby in a room with a smoky fire.

6. Things getting stuck in the throat

(a) Never prop up a baby's bottle so that it can feed on its own.

The milk can "go down the wrong way" and stop the baby breathing.

The teat can get stuck in the baby's throat.

Don't leave a baby with a small "little drink" bottle.

(b) Never leave an older baby to eat alone. Food can get stuck in its throat and choke it.

NEVÉR leave baby alone with a bottle

Cut food very small. Take out bones. Take all shell off egg.
(c) Don't leave any small things near a baby or small child which could get stuck in its nose or throat, e.g.

   Old dummies
   Beads
   Eyes of toys—take them out and embroider eyes on
   Buttons, fasteners, etc.
   Any fluffy material, fringes on covers, etc.

(d) Don't let small children have large or small hard sweets.
     It's safer not to let very little children have any of these things:

   Nuts
   Grated carrot (raw)
   Coconut
   Stringy food
   Skin, e.g. of fruit, baked beans, etc.
   Gluey sweets, e.g. chewing gum, toffees, big pieces of turkish delight, etc.

7. If a child has a cold or bad cough

(a) Keep an eye on him day and night.
(b) Try to keep him lying on one side.

 **Burns**

Every year many small children are burned to death. Many more are seriously ill for many months because they have been badly burned.

HOW DO CHILDREN GET BURNED?

Here are some ways:

1. By fires with no guard.

   (*a*) Children can fall right on the fire.
   (*b*) Their clothes can catch fire.
   (*c*) They throw paper, etc. into the fire.

2. By fires not guarded enough.

   (*a*) Sparks and bits of live coal can fall out and set fire to a child's clothes.
   (*b*) A child can still stick a long piece of paper or wood into the fire, or drop bits through the top of the guard if the holes are too big.
   (*c*) A portable fire can be knocked over.

3. By playing with matches, candles, etc.
4. By turning stoves on.
5. By fires caused by candles and night-lights.
6. From cigarettes.
7. From fires and fireworks on November 5th.
8. By being left unprotected in the hot sun too long.

HOW TO PREVENT children getting burned

Preventing children getting burned is made extra hard because:

(*a*) Many portable fires are not child-proof.
(*b*) Good guards are quite dear to buy.
(*c*) Children like playing with fire.

It is always the duty of adults to do all they can to prevent children getting burned, and there are laws to enforce this.

How to do it?

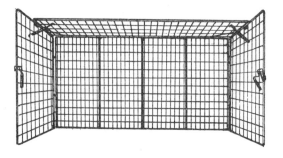

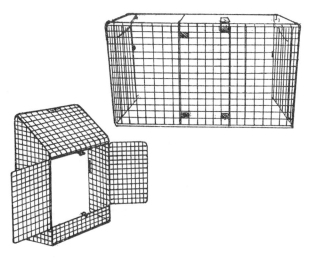

Three types of fireguard. Look for one that locks in place, with a "door" that enables the fire to be attended to without removing the guard

1. Fires

(a) Every fire must have a guard.
The guard must be:

Fixed so that a child can't undo it.
Fine enough to prevent:

Sparks coming through
Children poking sticks through.

Not so close to the fire that a child can get itself or its clothes burnt by touching it.

This means that many fires with guards already on them need an extra guard for real safety.

NOTE—Local Authorities will sometimes lend guards where there are small children, old or handicapped people and a guard can't be afforded.

(b) Toddlers should never be allowed to switch fires on, they are sure to do it when they are alone.

(c) Portable fires must be put in the safest place.

They must have an extra guard if needed.

Children must never be left in a room with an oil stove standing in it. This can be a hard rule to keep, but the child's life and the lives of the rest of the family may depend on it.

(d) Extra care must be taken:

If a child is taken to a house where the fire has no guard.
If you have no children, no extra guard and a child visits you.

(e) Adults should never do these things in front of children:

Throw paper, etc., on to a fire.
Light paper at a fire.

One day the child will do it too.

(f) A child must NEVER be left in a room when the fire is unguarded, e.g.

When it is being lit
When it is being made up or safe for the night.

2. Candles and night-lights

If these are used in a child's bedroom or anywhere else they must be:

Out of a draught
Firmly fixed
Standing in something which won't burn, with water in it too.
Out of a child's reach.

3. Matches and lighters

(a) Matches must always be kept out of a toddler's reach.

(b) It is dangerous to teach very little children how to "light Daddy's lighter".

4. Stoves

(a) Safety taps are a must, especially if burners light when the gas tap is turned.

(b) Battery lighters are safer than matches.

(c) The lighting guns on the sides of stoves are dangerous where there are toddlers. Children have been known to use these guns to set fire to curtains, etc.

5. Cigarettes

(a) Never smoke whilst holding a baby.

(b) Better not to smoke when playing with toddlers.

(c) Make extra sure that cigarettes and matches are quite out before putting them in ash trays. Small fingers do take them out sometimes.

Please don't smoke

6. November 5th

(a) Don't leave fireworks where small children can get them.

(b) Don't light fireworks too near children.

(c) Keep them away from the fire.

7. Clothes

(*a*) Use flame-proof materials for as many of the child's clothes as possible. Choose materials with a guarantee saying that the flame-resistant finish will last as long as the material.

(*b*) Nightdresses and party dresses **must** be made of flame-proof material.

But

(*a*) Still use a guard

(*b*) Wash exactly as the manufacturer says.

Note

There is more about safety from burning in the section on fire pp. 232–258 and in the section on buying, pp. 27–30.

8. Sun

(*a*) Don't leave babies unprotected in the hot sun at midday when the sun is hottest, even if they are already "brown".

(*b*) Best to put them in a shady place. If you use a sun canopy, keep an eye on the pram in case the baby gets exposed to the sun when the sun moves.

(*c*) Don't give them more than five to ten minutes sun-bathing a day before they get tanned. Then limit sun bathes to daily short periods.

(*d*) Keep an eye on toddlers on very sunny days:

Let them wear a thin loose cover-up garment for most of the time; probably a sun-hat too.

Make sure they play in the shade or indoors for part of the day.

Hurting Little Children

Little children may be hurt:

Physically
Mentally
Emotionally

Many of these injuries are not really accidents.
Some people hurt small children because they themselves are:

Jealous
Cruel
In a temper

Other people do it because:

They are careless.
They haven't enough patience.
They don't **know** how to look after children.
They are physically, mentally or emotionally ill.

It is up to everybody to do all they can to prevent little children from being hurt.

1. Be careful whom you leave little children with, e.g.

(a) Child minders, unless you are sure they will look after the child properly.
(b) Don't leave little babies alone with a young child.
(c) If any of the family are really jealous of, or really dislike, a child, don't leave the child in their care.
(d) Be careful about leaving small children with very aggressive or spiteful children.

2. Hitting little children

(a) Babies should never be hit.
(b) Children must never be hit where it might cause real damage, e.g. about the head.
(c) Never hit a child when you are in a temper.
(d) A child must never be punched, kicked, or hit with a hard object.

Many children grow up to be good adults without ever being hit.

3. Handling little children

Sometimes they get badly hurt by being treated roughly when they are:

Bathed
Dressed
Fed
Played with.

Although they often need to be handled firmly, the handling should always be gentle.

4. Understanding babies

It must always be understood that babies **never** do anything
Out of naughtiness
To be annoying
Out of spite, etc.

e.g. When they:

Cry
Refuse food
Dirty nappies or beds
Are sick
Stay awake.

5. Learning child care

Everybody who has the care of a child must know how to do it properly.

People who have brought up their own children well can be a great help to new parents.

Other good sources of help are:

Clinics
Doctors
Midwives
Health visitors
Mother care lessons at school
Parentcraft courses at evening school
Books.

6. Ill health

Sometimes people become impatient and even unkind to little children because they are physically, mentally, or emotionally ill themselves.

If anybody who has the care of small children finds themselves becoming less and less able to cope they should go to a doctor **before** things get really bad.

Sometimes they don't realise what is happening and need somebody else to tell them tactfully.

7. Cruelty and neglect

Where little children are being really cruelly treated in any way, help can be got from:

N.S.P.C.C. (The National Society for the Prevention of Cruelty to Children)
Child welfare centres
The police (in an emergency).

but somebody has to let them know.

Illness

Keeping little children safe from illness is as much a parent's responsibility as keeping them safe from accidents.
Parents should know

1. How to prevent as much illness as possible.
2. How to tell, and what to do, if a child becomes ill.

Help can be got from:

Doctors
Clinics
Health visitors
Midwives
    etc.

1. HOW TO PREVENT CHILDREN BECOMING ILL

The main ways of doing this are:

(a) Protecting them from infectious diseases.
(b) Keeping all the health rules.

Infectious diseases

Little children can become very ill or die if they get:

Smallpox
Diphtheria
Tetanus
Whooping cough
Measles
Tuberculosis
Poliomyelitis.

They can be kept safe from these illnesses by being vaccinated or inoculated against them.

Doctors and clinics will tell parents the best time to take the child to be done.

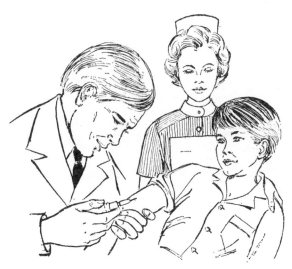

Immunization is wise and doesn't really **hurt**

Health rules

These include:

All the general ways of keeping the family healthy.
See p. 174 onwards.
Plus the extra care needed to keep small children healthy regarding—

Food
Cleanliness
Happiness.

Food

(*a*) Babies' and small children's food must always be **fresh, clean** and **covered**.

(*b*) All utensils used to prepare and serve the food must be perfectly clean.
This includes bottles and teats.

(*c*) Anybody touching a baby's food or feeding babies must:
Wash their hands and clean their nails first
Never sneeze or cough on the food or baby. Safer to wear a mask.

(*d*) Older babies must not be able to get at food which has been put in the rubbish bin or put down for dogs and cats.

(*e*) Babies and small children must have the right kind of food plus extra vitamins, e.g.

Vitamin C—Orange joice, Rose hip syrup
Vitamins A and D—Cod liver oil.

But get advice from clinic or doctor about how much to give.

Cleanliness

Everything to do with small children, especially babies, must be kept very clean.

(*a*) The baby himself must be kept clean, e.g.

Clean napkins when necessary
Buttocks washed
Sick cleared up quickly
Eyes, ears, nose, mouth cleaned gently.

(*b*) Clothes, bedding, toys, dummies, etc., must be kept clean.
(*c*) Potties and lavatories must be kept clean and germ free.

Happiness

Little children who are happy and contented are healthier than those who are not.
Besides being well looked after, children need a little extra attention daily, e.g.

Babies need to be nursed
Toddlers need to be played with and talked to

All little children need to feel **loved** and **wanted**.
They should never be left alone for hours and hours at a time every day.

Note

It is not safe to let strangers fuss and kiss babies, in case the person has a cold or other infection.

It is not safe for anybody with a cold to kiss little babies even on the forehead.

2. IF A CHILD BECOMES ILL

Parents must be able to recognize signs of illness in small children. Some signs which can be noticed are:

Loss of appetite
Excessive crying
Twitching
Stools which have blood or mucus in them, or which are loose
    and watery
Real sickness
High temperature for no apparent reason
Loss of weight
Rash
Unusual swellings
Coughs and sneezes
Sudden noisy breathing
Usually active toddlers becoming extra quiet for long periods
Changes in colour, e.g. extra pale or very flushed.

It is always wise to let a doctor see a child early if the child seems unwell, especially in cases of:

High temperature
Diarrhoea
Rash
Any sign of blood
Very young babies

Then do exactly what the doctor says.
Regular visits to a clinic are very useful because:

Signs of real illness can be discovered easily
Minor ailments can be put right and not allowed to drag on.

But

If the child is obviously ill it is better not to take it to the clinic but to call in the doctor.

 **Play**

If a child is to play safely he must

1. Have a safe place to play.
2. Have safe toys to play with (see p. 116).
3. Be watched all the time in some cases, e.g. very small children in garden paddling pools.
4. Be taught how to play safely.

A SAFE PLACE TO PLAY

It's a good idea to stand the playpen on a rug

Indoors

For very small children a play pen will be safest, but it must be put:

1. A safe distance from fires;
2. Away from anything which the child can grab at and get hurt, e.g.

    stoves in kitchen or living rooms
    tablecloths
      etc.

It is harder to make a safe play area indoors for toddlers, but it is safer if:

1. The part of the kitchen where the stove, etc. is can be fenced off with a low fence;
2. A "stable door" can be used instead of an ordinary door to the kitchen.

Safe and not solitary

The main thing is that small children should not be left **alone** to play in any room where they can hurt themselves.

Older babies must not be kept in a play pen all the time. There must be times when they can play outside the pen, watched of course.

In the garden

If a child is left alone to play in the garden, the garden must be safe.

1. The child must not be able to get through the fence or through the gate and into the road.

Safety features in a garden

2. There must be no poisonous plants in the garden (see p. 90).
3. The child must not be able to get into sheds containing tools, garden sprays and other dangerous things.
4. There should be no tools, broken glass, plant pots, etc. left about in the garden.
5. Paths and steps must be safe.

6. Any water must be firmly covered with wire netting, e.g.

Water butts
Fish ponds
Swimming and paddling pools.

7. Very small children must be within sight of the house all the time.
8. The child should not be able to play on any large equipment on its own if it could get hurt doing so, e.g. swings should be tied up when no adult is about.
9. Make sure they can't get at things in the dustbin.
10. Take extra care if you allow visiting children to play in the garden if it has not been made safe for children.

Outdoors

Many small children have no gardens to play in. The best that can be done for these children is:

1. See if there is somebody else's garden they can play in.
2. Try to make sure that they go to parks, recreation grounds or school playgrounds if this is allowed.
3. Make sure they are well trained in road safety.
4. Try never to let little children out to play alone.
5. That all road users should keep an eye open for children playing outdoors.
6. That parents should do their best to get a play place provided or at least a street cut off from traffic.

but as long as there is no safe place for small children to play in some areas, then every year many children will be killed or injured while "out to play".

Note

Farm machinery left unattended in fields may be dangerous. Children under 15 must not be allowed to ride on tractors; it is dangerous and illegal even if an adult is in charge.

TEACHING CHILDREN TO PLAY SAFELY

This must be done constantly but without too much fuss. How to do it?

This depends a lot on where the child plays, what toys he has, what he is like, etc., but some general rules are:

1. Teach him to use any toy properly if he could be hurt by using it the wrong way, e.g. carpenter's sets, etc.

2. Tidiness—not having all the toys out at once, especially big ones, e.g. if the bicycle is not being ridden, put it away instead of leaving it on the path.
   Also putting toys away when playing time is over.
3. Tell him to let you know if such things as bicycle brakes don't work, etc.
4. Teach them to share toys. This takes time! but a nasty accident can happen if a small child pushes the other one off the bike when he is riding it!
5. Obedience—small children must learn this about playing as much as with anything else if they are to play safely.
6. No rough play or messing about if a child is using or playing with something that could cause an accident. A stick, even a pen or pencil, poked in the face or fallen on, can do serious damage.
7. Children must be taught not to play with dangerous things used by an adult, e.g. a hatchet, a sporting rifle (even if you "know" the gun is not loaded). Guns must be unloaded and locked up after use.

Toys

Many little children are killed or badly hurt by toys. Most of these accidents need not happen if:

1. Only safe toys are bought
2. Only safe toys are given to children
3. Toys of older brothers and sisters are kept away from the little ones.

But

1. Many toys which are made for children are NOT SAFE.
2. Many safe toys can become dangerous if they are:

   (*a*) Broken
   (*b*) Badly mended
   (*c*) Not used properly
   (*d*) Given to younger children than they are made for.

When BUYING toys

1. Look for toys which are right for:

   (a) The child's age group
   (b) What he can do
   (c) What he is like.

2. Look for labels, e.g. the Kite Mark, saying the toy is:

   (a) Non-inflammable
   (b) Made of hygienic material
   (c) Painted with "lead free" paint.
      etc.

3. If there is no "safety label" ask somebody who really knows.
4. Use common sense.

Toys for small children must not be:

Too sharp
Too pointed
Too rough
Easily broken
Inflammable
Dangerous in any way.

Some firms take a lot of trouble to make their toys safe. They may be dearer to buy but it's better to buy a few of these than a lot of cheaper toys which may hurt a child.

Take extra care when buying foreign toys.

Here are some special points to watch for when buying toys:

Stuffed

e.g. Dolls, animals, teddy bears.

1. Check that the outside and inside of these toys is:

   (a) Not flammable
   (b) Hygienic—look for the seal of the Royal Institute of Hygiene.
   (c) Washable.

2. Make sure the eyes are firmly fixed or take them out and embroider eyes on.
3. Check that legs, arms, head and eyes are not fixed on with wire.

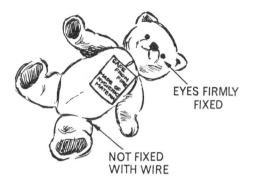

EYES FIRMLY
FIXED

NOT FIXED
WITH WIRE

Wood

This includes all kinds of toys played with mainly indoors as well as outdoor toys such as swings, slides, etc.

Check these toys for:

1. Splinters
2. Roughness, especially on the insides or underneath
3. Nails—nailed toys can always be dangerous. They are usually safer glued or screwed with screws which don't stick out.
4. Firm joints.

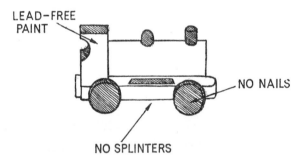

LEAD–FREE
PAINT

NO NAILS

NO SPLINTERS

Plastics

1. Toys made of brittle plastics usually have sharp edges when they break. This type is best avoided.
2. There are often small pieces which are meant to come off these toys, but small children can swallow "the little man". So don't buy for small children the toys with parts that come off. (Or you can remove them quietly some time!)

3. Plastic foam toys are not safe if the frame is stuffed with wire. You can usually feel it.

Tin

Tin is used for quite a lot of toys as well as parts of toys or boxes to put toys in, e.g. paintboxes, etc.

It is safer to feel the toy all over to make sure it has no sharp edges or corners before letting a child have it.

Electric

These toys are usually meant only for older children, but they are often played with on the floor where toddlers and babies are crawling.

To keep the little ones safe:

1. Try not to let the older ones play with electric toys where the little ones are.
2. Don't buy a toy rated at more than 20 volts. Enquire of an assistant who knows.

Mechanical

These are not safe for very small children to be left alone with, although they love to watch them "go".

When buying these toys, make sure:

1. that any part that has to be held won't hurt a child's hand.
2. that clockwork motors are enclosed.

Painted

As so many toys are painted and most small children suck toys at some time, it is very important that the paint should be harmless.

It is the LEAD in some paints which is so dangerous.

When buying painted toys make sure to ask if the paint is safe.

The British Standards Institution have a regulation regarding lead in the paint on toys.

It is therefore safer to buy toys which conform to this regulation.

Riding toys

These toys must be really strong, partly because some children are much heavier than others and partly because children like riding two at a time!

They must also:

1. Be well balanced
2. Have proper brakes or a control stick for adults to hold.

Home-made toys

As well as making sure all bought toys are safe it is important to make sure all HOME-MADE toys are safe.

This means:

1. They must be made of safe materials, e.g.

     Right kind of wood (which won't splinter easily).
     ˌFabric which won't flare up.

2. They must be finished properly inside and out.
3. If they are painted, that "left over paint" will not do if it is a lead type paint.
4. All the points regarding safety in bought toys must be watched when making toys.

     It is usually better to try to make only simple toys which are safe, unless the handyman is a real craftsman!

Notes

1. Most toys break sometimes whether they are bought or home made.

     It is important to:

     (*a*) Check toys often
     (*b*) Make sure the mended toy will be quite safe or throw it away (tactfully!)

2. It's always wise to keep an eye on toys which are brought in by other children.

 Outdoors

General rules for keeping small children safe outdoors are:

1. It is never really safe to let them out alone.

(*a*) Little children have been killed right outside their own homes.
(*b*) They have even been killed whilst somebody watched them "just go down the road".

2. When out in a pram or push chair they should

(*a*) Be strapped in so that they can't get out, and can't get strangled by the straps either.

(*b*) Not be left outside shops, libraries, etc. unless there is a reliable person to keep an eye on them.

Always make sure the brake is on and be extra careful if the ground slopes at all.

3. To prevent them getting really lost

(*a*) Make sure they have their name and address sewn on a garment they are not likely to take off, or wear an identity bracelet.

(*b*) Teach them to say their name and address as soon as possible.
(*c*) Use a leading rein when the child is really small.
(*d*) Teach them always to hold the hand or coat of the person they are with and to keep close.

4. On pavements

(*a*) Always let them walk on the inside.

(*b*) If small children are on a tricycle or in a toy car, it's safer to use a guiding stick. It's safer that they should learn to ride in a park or garden.

(*c*) It's better if little children don't have control of the dog's lead.

(*d*) Teach them not to stroke strange dogs, especially in hot weather.

5. On roads

(*a*) Whoever is taking the child out must always use proper crossings. ("Lights" and "zebras".)

(*b*) The person in charge of the child must always do kerb drill at crossings too!

(*c*) Every small child must be taught his kerb drill like this:

> Halt at the kerb
> Look right
> Look left
> Look right again,
> If all clear, walk straight across.
> (Make sure he understands "right" and "left".)

(*d*) Teach him that policemen, policewomen and traffic wardens are his friends and to cross roads near them when possible.

(*e*) Teach him never to cross near buses, cars, etc. that are standing still. This is important regarding the family car in the drive, too, **and** ice cream vans.

6. Public transport, etc.

(*a*) Little children must always be held when getting on and off trains and buses.

This is sometimes difficult if a mother has more than one small child, but other people will usually help.

(*b*) The child must also be held when:

> Getting in and out of lifts
> Going through swing or revolving doors
> Getting on and off and riding on escalators.

(*c*) Keep children away from platform edges.

(*d*) When queueing for buses don't let the child stand on the kerb side.

7. In cars (see p. 212)

Other outdoor safety rules are

(*a*) Teach children not to eat anything off the ground.

(*b*) When the child starts school:

First, take him and collect him for as long as necessary. Second, make sure he really knows and does his kerb drill. (Watch him once or twice when he can't see you.)

(*c*) When he starts going alone on buses or trains, make sure he knows general safety rules of travelling. See p. 208.

(*d*) Enrol him in the "TUFTY CLUB" started by the Royal Society for the Prevention of Accidents. The address is on p. 280.

(*e*) Never let children think zebra crossings are MAGIC!

(*f*) It's safer if children are not allowed to play with balls in the street (but difficult to make them obey!)

Note

Parents waiting outside school gates should not take up all the pavement so that children have to step into the road to pass.

 # Teaching Children Safety

As well as making their home, the things they use and the things they wear as safe as possible, children must be **taught** safety.

(*a*) To keep themselves safe

(*b*) To keep others safe.

HOW AND WHEN TO TEACH

Start as soon as they begin to crawl! E.g., take trouble to point out things which are hot and say the word "hot" to the child.

Older toddlers can be shown (carefully) hot things, but never put their fingers on or in anything hot, to "teach" them.

Teaching small children to obey safety words is rather like teaching a puppy. Just use single words,

e.g. "Down" is better than "Get down or I will smack you".

The words "hot", "down", "mind", "don't touch", "stop" (for

outdoors) are about all that will be needed to start with. When they obey, say "good boy" or "good girl".

As they get older, children soon learn the family safety language of words, actions and looks.

The important things to remember are:

(*a*) Small children CANNOT keep themselves safe.

(*b*) Older people must keep them safe ALL THE TIME.

This means that teaching must go on ALL THE TIME too!

By the way, don't tell children things if they aren't true, just to stop them doing something, e.g. "You'll fall down a big hole if you go down that road", or "Don't touch that, it burns", or "Don't drink that, it's poison".

If you do keep saying things are dangerous when they are not, children will not take any notice when you tell them not to do something that really is dangerous. Then they will get badly hurt or even killed.

The last point is about FEAR.

Fear is a child's natural protection **but** if you **terrify** him by shouting, he may get too scared to move and the accident you were trying to avoid will happen.

Notes

1. Children forget quickly. They have to be taught the same thing over and over again.
2. Some days they can't learn anything.
3. Too many "nos" without explanation will mean the child will do dangerous things behind your back.
4. Too much overprotection of older children will either turn them into "dare-devils" or make them too nervous to take care.
5. Don't try to teach too much at once, teach "bit by bit".
6. Many safety lessons need practice, e.g. home fire drill.
7. Teaching safety is not a quick or easy job. It takes lots of time and patience.
8. Always remember that the thing to aim at, is that in the end the child will be able to "do it himself".
9. Children can learn better from someone they love and trust.
10. Children will keep themselves safer if they feel loved and important.

WHAT TO TEACH

Here are a few general things to teach, but day to day living will probably produce quite a lot more!

1. Behaviour

The child who doesn't behave properly will usually have or cause many more accidents than one who does.

Obedience —This must be taught from the beginning. Safety training begins here.

Self-Control—Anybody who loses their self-control is likely to cause an accident to themselves or others.

Children must be taught to control temper, impatience, excitement, etc.

Selfishness —The child who always wants his own way and won't share anything often turns into the kind of driver, for instance, who won't give way and won't share the road.

"Manners" —Pushing, grabbing, bursting into rooms, shouting rude things, etc. all cause accidents.

Kindness, politeness, consideration, etc. all prevent accidents.

Gobbling food may well result in choking.

A place for his toys

2. Habits

Tidiness—

Accidents happen every day because things are either not put away or put away carelessly.

Small children should be taught as soon as they can crawl about to put things away in a big box or cupboard at the end of the day.

Older children must be taught to work and play reasonably tidily and put things away when finished with.

Taking things—

If children are taught not to take each other's things, younger children are not so likely to get hurt by older children's knives, chemistry sets, etc.

Touching things—

Small children like to feel everything. Teach them not to when it may be dangerous and save burns, cuts, bites, etc., etc.

Picking things up in the street—

Danger lies in picking up dangerous things, glass, etc., and in eating dangerous things.

3. Self-reliance

Children need a lot of extra safety care these days because there are so many dangers, but sooner or later, they have to learn to stand on their own feet and think and do things for themselves.

It's good for children to learn to do things for themselves

It is important to give them their freedom bit by bit as they are ready for it, but still to keep a quiet eye open for danger.

4. How to use dangerous things

If ever a child has to use a dangerous thing, he must

(*a*) Be shown how to use it safely
(*b*) Not be allowed to use it until he can do so safely.

Some things are too dangerous to let a child use even if he can, e.g. a child doesn't need to be very old to be able to drive a car but it wouldn't be safe to let him do so.

There are some dangerous things children can do if they are watched, but you have to make sure they won't or can't do them when alone.

Copying—
A child always copies the way grown-ups do things. This means that it is important that grown-ups always do things the safest way.

e.g. **Do** use an oven cloth
Don't use strips of paper to take a light from cookers, fires, etc.

Model sets

These are excellent for teaching safety, e.g. cooking, sweeping, ironing, laundry, tools, and gardening sets.

Use them to teach all the safety rules, e.g.

"Dry hands before ironing"
"Hold knives point downwards when carrying, etc."
"Hands behind the cutting edge" and "cut away from yourself".
"Strike matches away from yourself". Blow them out properly.
"Always **sweep** up broken glass".

Note—Never give a child a set which is far too advanced for his age.

Sweep up broken glass—don't pick it up

Later, children can be taught to use real tools, knives, etc., but they must

(*a*) Be told what can go wrong
(*b*) Be told to tell you if something is wrong or in some cases what to do
(*c*) Be taught the correct way of using the things
(*d*) Be taught to work carefully
(*e*) Be taught to practise until they have become really skilful
(*f*) Not to use certain things without permission
(*g*) Never to **play** about with dangerous things.

5. How to recognize danger

Children must be taught how to **know** when danger is around

(*a*) In the home and garden
(*b*) Outdoors.

They must be taught

(*a*) Which things are dangerous
(*b*) What accidents can happen
(*c*) Any information about the thing which will help (girls need to know things too).
(*d*) To tell you if there is anything wrong.

Older children must be taught safety care for the younger ones, e.g.

Fire rules
Water rules
Poisoning—not to give them and not to let them eat or drink anything that Mother doesn't know about.

"Signs and symbols"

Even small children can be taught to recognize and tell you danger signs such as

Smoke
Smell of gas
Crackling or sparking electric fires
Coal falling out of the fire
Heaters falling over
    etc.

As soon as they can read they must be taught which words mean danger and what kind of danger, e.g.

Danger	Poison
Fire	"For external use only"
High Voltage	"Not to be taken"
Inflammable	"Caution"

And, of course, the general use of the colour RED for dangerous things.

6. Going out to play

The first rule they must be taught is to always tell somebody in the family

(a) Where they are going
(b) What time they will be in

and also to send a message if they will be late. In the case of younger children **you tell them**, of course!

Dangers of the area:

(a) They must be told which these are
(b) They must be told how to manage them,

e.g. In some cases to "keep away".

Water—teach them to swim and float
　　　　Keep away from reservoirs
Woods—teach them how to find direction
　　　　　　　　how to climb trees
　　　　　　　　how to fall, i.e. to "go loose"
Main roads and level crossings—Make sure they know how to manage these before they go out alone

(See also p. 122.)

Pylons　　　　—If they touch the wires at the top they can get electrocuted.
　　　　　　　　If they nearly touch the wires they can get electrocuted.
　　　　　　　　If model aeroplanes touch the wires they can get electrocuted.
　　　　　　　　If kites (especially if the string is damp) touch the wires they can get electrocuted.
Electric trains —If they climb up to the overhead wires and touch them they can get electrocuted.
　　　　　　　　If they only nearly touch the wires they can get electrocuted.

If they climb on the tops of trains and don't touch the wires they can get electrocuted.

Building sites —Keep away is the best rule.

Derelict houses—Keep out.

Road works   —Danger lies in:

Holes—falling in them and getting covered with loose earth.

Bricks—and all kinds of things falling.

Walls—Old ones quite often fall and injure or kill children.

Lorries—Back out—and the driver can't see children.

Concrete mixers—It has happened that a child has fallen in and been killed.

Weather   —The danger here is mainly mist, fog and storms, particularly if the child is new to the area.

These are only a few danger spots, but parents should know at least the main danger spots of their area and either warn children about them or forbid them to go near.

Another important danger to warn children about in nearly any area is the danger of PICKING UP UNUSUAL things, e.g.

Bombs
Shells
Packets or tubes of pills.

The rules are

1. **Don't touch** anything suspicious.
2. **Don't eat** or **drink** anything you find.
3. Tell a policeman or parents if anything suspicious is seen about.

7. How to take risks

Whether parents like it or not, children are going to take risks.

The best thing to do is to teach them the safest way to do it such as:

"Ask yourself five things"

1. What danger is there?
2. Can I jump, swim, etc. that far?
3. What happens if I can't do it?
4. What can I do to prevent getting hurt if I fail?
5. Am I willing to have an accident? (At the least perhaps a broken leg and can't play in the football team.)

Summary

Children will be safer if:

1. They are obedient.
2. They can "give and take".
3. They are not treated as martyrs or heroes if they have an accident.
4. They are self-reliant—they can think for themselves.
5. They realise they can prevent accidents themselves. (Never blame the "naughty stove" for burning a child. He must realise **he** caused his burn, not the fire.)
6. They can recognize danger.
7. They are not frightened by safety teaching.
8. They get as much experience as possible, e.g. doing things, going places, meeting people.
9. They have plenty of safety knowledge, including how to get help.
10. They are encouraged to use any things they need such as glasses, hearing aids, etc.
11. They have all the safety skills, e.g. swimming.
12. Parents "keep up with things", know safety points and danger points of modern things, games, etc.

Organizations to help

St. John's Ambulance Brigade—Cadets
Red Cross—Junior section
Scouts
Duke of Edinburgh's Award scheme
Royal Society for the Prevention of Accidents—Tufty Club.

Old People

 ## Keeping Old People Safe

Old people are more likely to have accidents than younger people. This is because they can't do some things as well as they used to, e.g.

See, hear, smell
Move quickly
Lift or carry heavy things
Bend or stretch
Go up or down stairs
Get in or out of beds or chairs
Save themselves if they fall
Remember things
See danger
Realise the speed of traffic
Get on and off buses.

The main accidents old people have are:
Falls
Burns and scalds
Gas poisoning
Getting run over.

Old people will be less likely to have accidents if:

1. They have always been careful.
2. Everything is made as safe as possible for them. (This includes all the general home safety rules too.)
3. They have, and use, glasses, hearing aids, etc., if they need them.
4. People in the home and outside the home do all they can to help to keep old people safe.

In order to help keep old people safe, other people have to:

1. Note any special accident spots in the old person's home, or where he goes out to.
2. Note any special accidents the old person is likely to have. For instance, if they can't see very well

   (a) They are more likely to be run over
   (b) They will bang into things, etc.

3. Be tactful. Old people's feelings are often easily hurt and they don't like feeling they are being treated like children.

HERE ARE SOME WAYS to help keep old people safe:

1. Burns

Many old people are burnt to death every year.
Here are some of the causes:

(a) Falling on to coal and other fires.
(b) Their clothes or bedclothes catching fire from fires or cigarettes.
(c) Oil stoves being knocked over.
(d) Candles.
(e) Gas rings.

What can be done?

(a) All fires should be as safe as possible. Radiators are better than most kinds of fire.
(b) All fires must be very well GUARDED.
(c) Armchairs and beds should not be too close to a fire.
(d) If possible old people should not:

   Light or make up coal fires
   Light or fill oil stoves.

(*e*) They should have a good torch so that they don't need to carry candles about.

(*f*) If they smoke there should be plenty of large deep ashtrays, especially by beds and armchairs.

(*g*) As much as possible of their clothing, bedclothes and furnishing materials should be made of non-flare fabrics.

But

It is not easy to keep old people safe from fire because

(*a*) They have been used to managing fires all their lives.

(*b*) They often live alone.

(*c*) Many of them haven't the money to get safer fires, guards, clothes, etc.

2. Scalds

Old people can easily be scalded by hot water, tea, etc. if:

(*a*) Their hands tremble.

(*b*) They are still using the large kettles, etc. that they used when all the family was at home.

(*c*) Bath water is run too hot.

Bad scalds can be prevented if:

(*a*) They are not handed scalding hot cups of tea.

(*b*) They have small pans, kettles, and teapots if they live alone.

(*c*) Baths are run for them. Cold water before hot. (It's always safer to stay around when old people are bathing.)

(*d*) Hot water bottles are in good repair and are filled for them. (Don't make them too hot. Do put a cover on.)

(*e*) Handles of pans and spouts of kettles are not sticking out over the edge of the stove or gas ring where they can be knocked.

3. Gas poisoning

Old people are very likely to be poisoned by gas for these reasons:

(*a*) Their sense of smell may not be very good or they may not be able to smell at all.

(*b*) They are sometimes forgetful. They may turn a gas tap on, then go and do something else and forget to light the gas.

(*c*) If a gas blows out they may not smell the escaping gas.

(*d*) If they are very lonely, miserable or depressed.

It is most important where there are old people that somebody should do these things for them:

(a) Make sure all gas fittings are safe. The Gas Board will do this.

(b) Make sure all gas appliances are safe. The Gas Board will check them.

(c) Ask the Gas Board if they have any safety devices for old people.

(d) Check that gas taps are off at night.

(e) Make sure there is at least a little ventilation in any room where gas appliances are used.

(f) Give old people a flask of tea for the night so that they need not light gases to boil water.

(g) Be always alert (but don't nag) to the smell of gas.

4. Falls

When old people fall they usually hurt themselves more than younger people do when they fall.

This is because:

(a) They can't save themselves.

(b) Their bones are brittle and break easily.

They suffer from shock more, too.

The house which has been made safe as possible to prevent people falling will be safer for old people too, e..g.

(a) Nothing to trip over on floors and stairs.

(b) No slippery floors or stairs.

(c) Good lighting including easy to switch on bedside lamps.

(d) A handrail on the wall side of staircases or odd steps. Outlining step edges in white.

Some of the things which help to save small children from falls will help very old people too, e.g.

(a) Bars on high windows
(b) A gate at the top of the stairs
(c) A non-slip mat or towel in the bath.

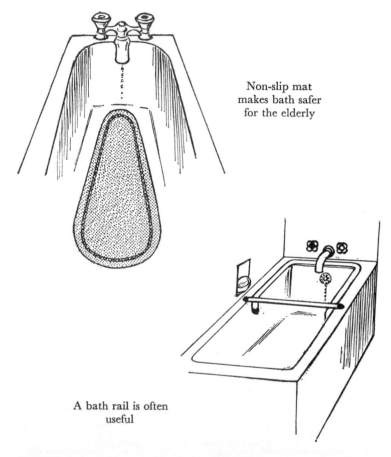

Non-slip mat
makes bath safer
for the elderly

A bath rail is often
useful

A few extra things which can be done to save old people from falling are:

(a) Encouraging them to use a stick if they can't walk very well.
(b) Trying to prevent them climbing on chairs and ladders.
(c) Taking very old people out for walks instead of letting them go out alone.

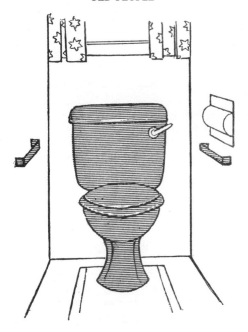

(*d*) A handrail on the wall of the lavatory and beside bath.

(*e*) Making sure beds and chairs are the right height so that the old person won't have an accident trying to get up and down. (Chairs should have a soft edge to prevent too much pressure on legs.)

(*f*) Having a chair instead of a stool in the bathroom.

(*g*) Rubber tips on walking sticks.

(*h*) NEVER rush them.

(*i*) Don't put their things on very high shelves.

5. Road accidents

A large number of old people get run over and are killed crossing roads.

There are many reasons for this.

Here are some:

(*a*) They can't see very far and don't see traffic coming.

(*b*) They can't see things "out of the corner of their eye".

(*c*) They can't judge the speed of cars.

(*d*) They can't turn their heads quickly.

(*e*) They can't hear things coming.

(*f*) They can't walk quickly.

Another important reason why old people get run over is because they don't understand traffic and traffic systems, e.g.

(a) One way streets—they don't expect cars to come at them on what seems to be the wrong side of the road.

(b) They can't always understand traffic lights, especially in one way streets.

(c) They think nothing can run over them if they are on a crossing and just walk across sometimes without looking to see if anything is coming.

(d) They don't realise that cars need enough distance to pull up in.

(e) They don't realize that not all drivers obey the rules of the road.

What is the answer to old people's road problems?

(a) Road safety rules should be explained to them, especially new ones.

(b) Really old people should have somebody with them when they go out.

(c) It's up to everybody to be ready to help an old person across a road. Often the best way is to say nothing and just "happen" to cross in the same place unless it is a very dangerous spot.

(d) All drivers should be extra careful if they see an old person crossing or about to cross the road.

Some general ways of helping to keep old people safe

1. Medicine—It's best to give old people their medicine, especially if they are forgetful or can't read easily.

   This is very important regarding sleeping pills. Their medicine must be labelled carefully in large letters in case they take it themselves.

2. Burglars—Somebody should make the old person's home safe from burglars, especially if the old person can't hear well, e.g. a safety chain on front and back doors.

3. Food—If an old person cannot see or smell well they can, and do, eat bad food which may kill them.

   A fridge or somebody to check the food they eat is very necessary.

4. Signals—A bell near the chair or bed will enable an old person to call for help in an emergency.

   An "S O S" card or flashing light to put in the window can save lives.

   A telephone is really a necessity for old people living alone.

5. Going out—

    (*a*) They should always have their name and address on them.

    (*b*) If they have to come home late at night somebody should be with them.

    (*c*) They should always have a little money on them.

    (*d*) They should not carry valuables around.

6. Electric blankets—These should be switched on and off for them.

7. Small children—

    (*a*) It isn't really safe to leave a very old person in charge of toddlers.

    (*b*) Very old people should not go further than they can be seen with babies in prams.

Tactful help for older people

8. Heavy weights—

 (*a*) Old people shouldn't carry heavy weights, e.g. coal.
 (*b*) They shouldn't have to move heavy furniture.

9. Salesmen—It is often safer if old people don't open the door to these.

 They should also tell the police if a salesman tries to force them to buy things.

Accidents

What to do

It is important to know what to do BEFORE accidents happen.

1. At least one person in the family should have done a FIRST AID course—best if they all do.
2. Everybody should know how to give artificial respiration.
3. Everybody should know how to stop bleeding.
4. Everybody should know how to treat fainting.
5. It is important to know how to get help quickly:

    (*a*) Quickest way to hospital
    (*b*) Where the CASUALTY entrance is
    (*c*) Nearest telephone if you haven't one
    (*d*) Doctor's telephone number
    (*e*) Taxi number
    (*f*) Which neighbour will help in an emergency.

6. Every home should have these things:

    FIRST AID kit
    FIRST AID book

General rules

1. Remove person from source of accident, e.g. from fireplace.

In bad accidents only move if the person is likely to get hurt more if they are not moved.

2. Give artificial respiration if breathing has stopped.
3. Get help quickly—you may need to send somebody else to get help, neighbours, passers-by, anybody.
4. Stop bleeding.
5. All accidents cause some shock or fright.

Remember:

(*a*) To comfort the person—especially children.
(*b*) Don't leave them alone if you can help it.
(*c*) Never scream, cry or fuss in any way.
(*d*) Don't move the person more than is necessary.
(*e*) Handle the person gently.

6. Don't let people crowd around.
7. Loosen clothes but don't **take them** off unless necessary.
8. Don't give alcohol.
9. Don't give food or drink in cases of bad accidents (except a drink for burns—if the person is conscious).
10. Let the person help themselves too, e.g. press on a cut to stop bleeding **but** don't let them do anything which may cause them more injury.

Notes

1. DON'T do anything if you don't know how to do it. You might do more harm than good.

   One of the worst things in the case of an accident is not being able to do anything to help. The only answer is to learn FIRST AID BEFOREHAND.

2. The doctor will often tell you on the phone what FIRST AID to give before he comes.

3. When outside the home everybody should have these things on them:

   (*a*) Name, address, any telephone number
   (*b*) Name, address and telephone number of any person who can be contacted in case of accident.
   (*c*) Any important medical information, e.g.:

   Special blood group
   If diabetic
   Allergies to medicines.

An identity bracelet is the safest way to carry this kind of information.

Burns and Scalds

Treatment for scalds is much the same as for burns, but there will not be flames to put out.

CLOTHES ON FIRE

1. Pull person away from fire.
2. Roll person in mat, blanket or coat (head out) until flames are out. (Don't get your own clothes on fire.)
3. Take to CASUALTY department of Hospital ⎫
   Or Call ambulance   ⎬ whichever is
   Or Call doctor   ⎭ quickest.

If person is conscious, give them tea with sugar, or water to keep sipping until they get to hospital. Add ½ teaspoon salt and a good pinch of bicarbonate of soda to the water.

CARRY GENTLY

OTHER BAD BURNS

1. Remove person from heat, e.g.

    (*a*) Pull away from fire
    (*b*) Pull out of boiling liquid
    (*c*) Take hot coal off them.

2. Take to CASUALTY department of hospital ⎫
   Or Call ambulance   ⎬ whichever is
   Or Call doctor   ⎭ quickest.

If person is conscious, give them water (as above) to keep sipping until they get to hospital.

NOT SUCH BAD BURNS

Smaller than a halfpenny
Skin red or blistered (not deeply burned)

1. Wash your hands.
2. Hold burnt part under cold tap or pour cold water on it (gently).
3. Put one of these on the burn

    (*a*) Special burn dressing

(*b*) Cover burn with paraffin gauze, then bandage, or clean cotton or linen. (Don't use fluffy material.)

4. Let doctor see the burn if it does not heal properly.
5. Best to let doctor see any burns on babies.

IMPORTANT

Don't touch burns. NEVER try to "wipe them clean".

Don't put on any of these things:

Ointment
Lotion
Flour
Fat
Soap

Don't pull off clothes sticking to burns **unless** the clothes are soaked in oil, petrol, acid or alkali.

Don't open burn blisters.

Don't breathe on burns.

WAITING

If you have to wait for help, keep pouring (gently) cold water over the burnt part. Then gently cover with burn dressing or clean cotton or linen.

Remember

When people are badly burned or scalded they get shocked and frightened too, especially small children (see p. 153 for Shock).

Note

1. Make a note of any new treatments for burns.
2. If the burn is deep, however small, a doctor should see it.
3. If the burn is not deep but covers a large area, the doctor should see it.
4. Any burns on the eye, however small, should be seen by a doctor.
5. If acids or alkalis go in the eye:

   (*a*) Lay the person down—bad eye side down.
   (*b*) Pour cold water over the eye for ten minutes (use clock). Open the eyelids gently so that the water goes on the eyeball.
   (*c*) Get the person to hospital (Casualty department).

SUNBURN

Mild (no blisters)—Use special sunburn cream.
Bad—Call the doctor or take the person to the doctor.
> Give them water to keep sipping. Add $\frac{1}{2}$ teaspoon salt and a good pinch of bicarbonate of soda to the water.

 # Loss of Consciousness

Some of the reasons a person may become unconscious are:

General causes

Lack of fresh air
Lack of food
Malnutrition
Indigestion
Standing too long
Fright
Over-tiredness

Accident or illness

Severe pain
Loss of blood
"Weak heart"
"Stroke"

What usually happens

Face becomes pale or red
Skin cold and damp
Breathing shallow
Giddy feeling
Weak feeling
Collapse.

What to do

1. In cases of accident or illness

(a) Call a doctor or ambulance.
(b) Loosen clothes—collar, bras, belts, etc.

(c) Lay the person down on his side, face down. (If face is red, keep head up.)

(d) Cover them with a blanket.

(e) Check breathing—start artificial respiration if necessary.

If you can see where any blood is coming from:

(a) Press a pad of material on it. (Round it if there is glass etc. in it.) (Don't press on ears, just lay pad on.)

(b) When the pad is soaked in blood, don't take it off, but press another pad on top. (See also "Bleeding", p. 150.)

Don't give them food, drink, aspirin or alcohol when they come round.

Don't leave them alone.

Note

Look for any information, e.g. a card or bracelet stating that the person is diabetic, has fits etc.

2. General causes

(a) Loosen clothes

(b) If the person has fallen down—lay him flat, head on one side. If the person is sitting—bend his head down between knees. IF FACE IS RED, KEEP HEAD UP.

(c) Give fresh air—open window or fan the person.

(d) Put a blanket round him if it's cold.

(e) When they feel better, give a warm drink with sugar, if they like it. Don't give them aspirin or tablets with aspirin in them. Don't leave them alone.

Note

If the person takes a long time to come round or keeps fainting, send for the doctor.

HEART ATTACK

The usual signs are:

Shortness of breath
Pain in chest (may go down arms)
Falling down or clutching table, etc.

What to do

1. Send for the doctor.

2. Keep the person supported in a sitting position.
3. Loosen clothes at neck and waist.
4. Give them fresh air.
5. Cover with a blanket.
6. If you know the person has to have tablets, etc., if he has an attack, give him what he should have when he comes round.

STROKE

The usual signs are:

Person collapses
Face is red
Breathing noisy
One or both pupils of eyes become large
When they come to, may not be able to talk properly or move arms or legs.

What to do

1. Send for the doctor.
2. Keep head up.
3. Loosen clothes at neck and waist.
4. Wipe mouth—take out false teeth.
5. Cover with blanket.
6. Don't give food, drink or alcohol.
7. Keep person very still.

 Poisoning

Some of the usual ways of telling if a person has eaten or drunk something poisonous, apart from seeing them do it, are:

1. Burns round the mouth
2. Stomach pains
3. Sickness (sometimes with blood)
4. Diarrhoea
5. Unconsciousness
6. Sleepiness
7. Convulsions
8. Quick deep breathing
9. Very red face.

Whatever poison has been swallowed, somebody must

(*a*) Get the person to the hospital (Casualty department) at once.
(*b*) Take the container to the hospital and any left over tablets, etc.
(*c*) If the person has been sick, take some of this too (in a jar, plastic bag, etc.).

While you are waiting for help, if the person is very ill and is conscious, give plenty of water to drink. Apart from this, keep them lying on side to prevent vomit from choking them.

It is important to remember that

1. Sometimes a child is sick after swallowing poison and then **seems** all right.
2. Some poisons do not take effect for many hours after they have been taken.

In both these cases the child or adult must still be seen by a doctor **as soon as it is known** that poison has been swallowed.

Notes

1. If a child has eaten something which you think **may** be poisonous but you are not sure, play safe and let a doctor see the child straight away.
2. If a bottle, etc., contains less of poisonous substance than you think it should, check up quickly.
3. Look in a child's mouth for any unswallowed tablets.

 Electrocution

When a person is electrocuted:

Their muscles become paralysed so that—

(*a*) They cannot let go of or move away from the thing which has electrocuted them.
(*b*) They may fall away from the source of electrocution, e.g. from a ceiling light.

If they are still touching the source of electrocution:

(*a*) Electricity will still be running through their body.

(*b*) If anybody touches their body with bare hands, that person will be electrocuted too.

WHAT TO DO

1. If possible

Turn off electricity
Pull out plug

Then pull person away.

OR

2. Do one of these things—(Don't touch any water.)

(*a*) Pull person away by a loose part of their CLOTHES.
DO NOT TOUCH THEIR BODY at the same time.
Remember babies' nappies may be WET.
Don't touch parts of body which may be wet with perspiration, e.g. forehead and under arms.

(*b*) Push them away with anything made of WOOD, e.g.

chair
coffee table
walking stick (with no metal on it).

(*c*) Put on rubber gloves—MUST be DRY

Stand on rubber mat
Pull person away.

(*d*) Pull the appliance away by its flex. (Don't touch a frayed part and don't let the appliance bang against yourself.) Warn anyone near that the appliance is still live.

Notes

(*a*) If somebody else is in the house send them for a doctor or to ring 999.

(*b*) If you are alone:

Get the person away from the electricity first.
If breathing has stopped, give artificial respiration if you really know how.
Send for the doctor.

(*c*) Even if the person doesn't seem to be hurt much they should still be seen by a doctor, especially children.

Cuts, Scratches

A doctor is needed in all bad cases of the following:

Cuts
Stabs—by knives, nails, etc.
Scratches—from rusty nails
Scratches—from sick animals
When glass, etc., is embedded in flesh
All cuts, etc., done in the garden.

Either get person to hospital at once (Casualty department)
Or take to doctor or send for him.

Whilst waiting for the doctor

Bad bleeding

(a) Lay person down—cover with blanket.
(b) Raise cut arm or leg on cushion if not broken.
(c) Take out glass, etc. if this is easy.
(d) Press pad of clean material on wound. (If you can't find material quickly press with your hand, finger or thumb.)
(e) When pad is soaked in blood, press another pad on top of first pad.

If there is still glass or something else in the wound, press the flesh round the wound so that you don't press on the glass, etc.

Always treat for shock in cases of bad bleeding.

Small cuts, etc.

(a) Wash under running tap
(b) Pat dry with clean cotton or linen
(c) Put an adhesive dressing on.

If the cut does not heal properly a doctor should see it.

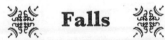 # Falls

HEAD

Must call the doctor if the person

Becomes unconscious

Bleeds from mouth, ears, nose
Is sick
Very sleepy
Can't eat
Has very bad headache
Stays very pale
Stays very irritable
Keeps feeling giddy.

Any of these things may happen

(*a*) At the time of the fall
(*b*) Within the next few days
(*c*) Even later in some cases.

Before the doctor comes

1. Very bad falls

    (*a*) Leave person where they are unless they are in further danger
    (*b*) Cover with blanket
    (*c*) Give artificial respiration if necessary
    (*d*) Stop any bleeding.

2. Other falls

    (*a*) Gently carry person onto bed or settee
    (*b*) Loosen clothes—don't undress
    (*c*) Cover with blanket
    (*d*) Pull curtains.

LEGS AND ARMS

If limb is:

Very painful
Can't be moved
In unnatural position
Very swollen
Very discoloured

Either take the person to hospital (Casualty department)
Or call the doctor.
Don't—move it round and round to "see if it's broken". If it is you will make the break worse.

Before the doctor comes

(*a*) Treat for any faintness and for shock.

(*b*) Leave person where they are if possible.
(*c*) If they must be moved, carry gently, supporting injured limb.
(*d*) Loosen clothes—don't undress.
(*e*) Undo shoe—only take off if not too painful.
(*f*) Cover with blanket.
(*g*) Don't give any food or drink, in case he needs an anaesthetic later.

Note

In all cases of

Falls from high places
Head bangs on stone, concrete, etc.
It's best to see the doctor even if
   The person feels all right
   No injury can be seen.

 # Bites and Stings

WHAT TO DO

1. Any of the following must be seen by a doctor at once or take the person to hospital (Casualty department).

  (*a*) Bites from

         Dogs
         Cats
         Birds
         Snakes
         Monkeys

  (*b*) Insect bites and stings:

      In or round Mouth
             Nose
             Eyes
             Ears
             Throat

      If person feels sick or ill after any insect bite or sting.
  (*c*) Plant sting, if person feels sick or ill from it.

2. Treat for shock (or fright) especially in little children.
3. In cases of mild insect bites or stings or plant stings, put on

Anti-histamine ointment or lotion ⎫
T.C.P. ⎬ Read directions first.
Dettol ⎭

If the sting has been left in—hold a needle in a flame until it is red hot, cool it, and remove the sting with it. Don't press the poison bag at the end of the sting or poison will go in the wound.

4. If the snake has been killed, take it to the doctor too!
5. Tell the person he is not going to die.

 # Varicose Vein (Burst)

1. Send for the doctor.
2. Lay person down. Remove garters and stockings.
3. Hold leg up high—use cushions or keep holding it.
4. Press pad of clean material where blood is coming from. When pad is soaked in blood, don't move it but press another pad on top.

 # Shock

Whenever a person is badly injured or badly frightened they are often said to suffer from shock.

Remember

(a) That babies and small children may suffer from shock following what may seem to a grown-up only small accidents or frights.

(b) People, especially little children, sick people and old people, can die if they are badly shocked.

(c) It's always wise to treat for shock in any accident even if the person doesn't seem shocked. Some people put on a bright air when they are hurt.

What usually happens

Face pale
Rapid, shallow breathing
Feels sick
Feels cold although sweat may show on forehead and round mouth
Shivering
Pulse very fast and weak
Faintness
Sometimes can't move at all
May become unconscious

SHOCK WITHOUT INJURY

Mild

1. Comfort the person.
2. Put them to rest on armchair or settee.
3. Put a blanket round them.
4. Give them a cup of tea with sugar (unless they refuse to drink it with sugar).
5. Don't leave them alone.

Bad

1. Send for doctor and ambulance.
2. Lay the person down with feet on a pillow, head on one side. (If they are sick, prop them up instead.)
3. Loosen their clothes (don't take them off).
4. Cover them up (no hot water bottles).
5. Give a warm drink if they want it (no alcohol). Tea with sugar, if they'll take it.
6. Comfort them.
7. Don't leave them alone.
8. You may have to treat for faintness or give artificial respiration.

SHOCK WITH INJURY

Mild

If both shock and injury are mild:

1. Comfort them.
2. Put them to rest on armchair or settee.
3. Put a blanket round them.
4. Give them a cup of tea with sugar if they'll take it (no alcohol).

5. Treat the injury.
6. Don't leave them alone.

If it's the sight of bleeding from a small cut that upsets them, stop the bleeding and cover it up quickly.

Bad

1. Send for ambulance and doctor.
2. If breathing has stopped, start artificial respiration (if you know how).
3. Stop bad bleeding (if you know how).
4. Loosen clothes—don't take them off.
5. Cover with blanket (no hot water bottles).
6. Don't give anything to drink.
7. Talk quietly and comfortingly if person is conscious.
8. If possible, lay person down with head low. Don't move more than necessary.

BABIES AND LITTLE CHILDREN

Treat as for adults except that if there is no bad injury and the child is conscious:

1. It's best to hold the child in your arms.
2. Give it warm, sweet milk or favourite drink.
3. Give it a doll, etc., to cuddle if you have to leave it, e.g. to warm the milk.
4. Don't talk about it afterwards unless the child does.
5. If the shock doesn't wear off fairly quickly, it's best to let doctor see child. (This applies to very old people too.)
6. Watch for return of fright in the night. (This applies to very old people too.)

 # Forms of Choking, Smothering, etc.

PERSON GASSED

If you suspect what has happened take a deep breath before you open the door, then:

1. Leave door open.

2. Open window wide. (Break glass if window won't open.) Take another breath.
3. Turn off gas.
4. Pull person out of room into fresh air.
5. Walk them around in the fresh air, if possible.
6. If they are unconscious, and

(*a*) You are alone—

If you don't know artificial respiration, send for ambulance and doctor.

If you do know artificial respiration, do it until person breathes again and then send for doctor.

(*b*) You are not alone—

One person can go for help whilst the other starts artificial respiration.

Notes

1. Don't light matches or smoke whilst gas is still about.
2. If you get the person "better" yourself, they should still be seen by a doctor.
3. Remember, the lips and skin of a gassed person look pink. They don't look grey and ill.

PERSON OVERCOME BY FUMES

Whether the accident occurs in the house or in a garage the treatment is the same.

1. Get the person into the fresh air.
2. Treat as for number 6 "person gassed".

SWALLOWED OBJECTS

Small smooth object

This is not usually dangerous.

(*a*) It will probably go through the child's body.
(*b*) Look out for it in his potty.
(*c*) Tell the doctor if you are worried.

Big object

1. Take the person to hospital (Casualty department) if they are not choking.

2. If they are choking:

(*a*) Tell them to cough hard.
(*b*) Get someone to call doctor or ambulance.
(*c*) If they are going blue and can't breathe—

Children—turn upside down on lap and slap between shoulders.
Adults —Take out false teeth. Bend their shoulders forward and thump between shoulder blades.
Or Try to hook it out with a finger. They may sick it up then.

Sharp object

e.g. pins, glass, fish bones, etc.

1. Take the person to the hospital (Casualty department).
2. Try to keep them calm.

STRANGULATION

1. Cut the rope if the person is hanging (to get them down).
2. Cut the rope or whatever is round the neck.

If you are alone:

(*a*) Send for ambulance or doctor if you don't know artificial respiration.
(*b*) Start artificial respiration if you know it.

If somebody is there:

One person can go for help whilst the other starts artificial respiration.

DROWNING

1. Get the person out of the water. Carry them so that water runs out of mouth.
2. If you are alone:

(*a*) Send for ambulance or doctor if you don't know artificial respiration.
(*b*) If you know artificial respiration—
Clear person's mouth of weeds, false teeth, etc.
Start artificial respiration (see p. 158).

Send for doctor as soon as person can breathe again.
Cover the person with blankets. (Keep them lying down,
on the side.)
Do anything doctor has said.

BABY SMOTHERED

1. Take the pillow or whatever it is off the child's face.
2. Send somebody for doctor and ambulance.
3. Start artificial respiration if you know how.

If you are alone—

Start artificial respiration if you know it.
When child starts to breathe, send for doctor.

If you don't know artificial respiration, send for doctor and
ambulance AT ONCE.

 # Artificial Respiration

The simplest method is to breathe into the person's lungs. There
are three ways to do this:

1. Breathe into their mouth (if their nose is blocked).
2. Breathe into their nose (if their mouth won't open).
3. Breathe into their mouth and nose at the same time (do this
for very small children).

The important things to remember are:

1. Don't waste any time—the person has only about five **minutes**
to live after they stop breathing. Do it on the spot.
2. Keep their head well back.
3. If you get them to breathe again on their own, watch to see if
they stop again. Begin again if they do.
4. Don't let them sit up when they start breathing. Keep them
lying down until the doctor comes.
5. If they are still unconscious when they have started to breathe
turn them on their side face down (see also p. 145).

You can tell if a person is not breathing:

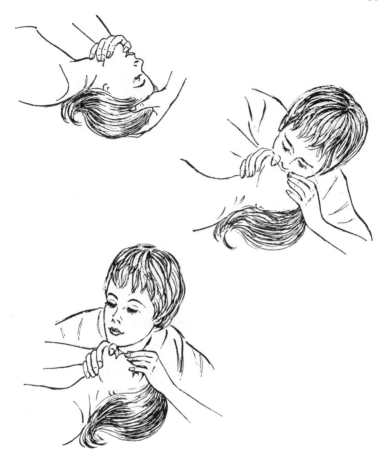

(a) By looking to see if their chest, or the part of their body just below their chest, is going up and down.

(b) By listening near their mouth.

The Mouth to Mouth Method

1. Lay the person on his back.
   Quickly take anything out of his mouth.
2. Put one hand on his forehead ⎫
   Put one hand under his chin ⎭ Press his head well back.
   Pinch his nose to close his nostrils.
3. Take a deep breath.
   Open your mouth wide.

Press your mouth over his mouth.
Blow into his mouth—watch his chest rise.
Take your mouth away.
4. Watch his chest fall—take a deep breath while watching.

Keep on doing 3 and 4 for at least an hour.

Or

(*a*) Until he starts to breathe himself.
(*b*) Until the doctor comes and says stop.

Note

For the Mouth to Nose Method do exactly the same, but

(*a*) Breathe into the person's nose.
(*b*) Pinch their lips shut.

Fits

BABIES

What usually happens:
Face may go white then blue
Body may twitch
Eyes may turn upwards
Mouth may froth.

What to do

1. Call the doctor

2. Lay the child down
3. Turn his head to one side
4. Cover him with a blanket
5. Stay with him.

If you are alone and can telephone the doctor yourself, lay the child on the floor if necessary to make sure you can still see him.

EPILEPTIC FITS

What usually happens:

The person falls down
Throws his arms and legs about
May froth at mouth
May wet themselves

WHAT TO DO

1. Call a doctor.
2. Move any furniture away from him.
3. Try to put a gag between the teeth, but

   Don't use anything too small in case it gets swallowed, and nothing hard that will break their teeth.
   Don't use force.

4. Try to slip a pillow under the person's head if the face is very red.

When the fit is over, put the person to bed with a hot water bottle in cold weather. Let them go to sleep.

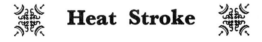

Heat Stroke

A person can get heat stroke whether he is out in the sun or working in a hot place.
The usual signs are:

Red face
Skin hot
Heart "banging"

Very high temperature
Weakness
Might become unconscious.

What' to do

1. Send for doctor.
2. Lay in cool place—head up.
3. Take all clothes off (outdoors—take off and loosen as much as possible).
4. Fan body.
5. Squeeze out flannel with cold water and wipe body all over.
6. If doctor hasn't come and person is conscious, give a glass of water or fruit drink (not fizzy) with a $\frac{1}{4}$ of a teaspoon of salt in it.

Body too cold

It is dangerous if a person's body gets too cold, especially in the case of babies and old people.

What happens?

Temperature gets very low (too low for an ordinary thermometer)
Pulse weak and low
Breathing shallow
Body feels very cold to touch
The person may become unconscious and die.

But the person may not LOOK cold.

What to do?

Send for the doctor
Wrap the person in blankets (best to warm babies against the mother's body as well)
Put them in a warm room
Give a warm sweet drink (if conscious).

Don't:

Put them too close to the fire
Use hot water bottles or electric blankets.

Eyes, Ears, Nose

EYES

1. If the eye is bleeding—DON'T TOUCH IT.
2. If there is glass or anything **sharp** in the eye—DON'T TOUCH IT.
3. If there is anything **hot** in the eye—DON'T TOUCH IT.

In all these cases:

(a) Don't let the person rub his eye.
(b) Take him to the hospital (Casualty department) or to the doctor at once.

4. Specks of dust in the eye:

(a) Damp the corner of a clean handkerchief.
(b) Try GENTLY to get it out.

If it won't come out with the GENTLEST touch, take the person to the hospital (Casualty department) or doctor.

5. Any cleaning liquids, etc. in the eye—keep running cold water into the eye, open eyelids so that eyeball gets properly washed. Take to hospital or doctor at once.

Remember

Even the smallest speck of dust can scratch the eye and cause serious injury.

EARS

(a) If the ear is bleeding—
(b) If anything at all has got into an ear—

In both cases take the person to the hospital (Casualty department) or to the doctor.

NOSE

1. Something pushed in it:

(a) Tell the person to breathe through mouth.
(b) Take them to the hospital (Casualty department) or doctor.

2. Bleeding:

(a) Sit person by open window. (Lay him down if he feels bad.)

(*b*) Loosen clothes at neck and chest.

(*c*) Tell person to breathe through mouth.

(*d*) Tell him to hold his nose (you do it for little child).

(*e*) Tell him not to blow his nose.

If the bleeding won't stop after about fifteen minutes, take him to the hospital (Casualty department) or to the doctor.

If an elderly person gets a nose bleed it's always best to send for the doctor.

 # When to call the Doctor

In most cases of minor accidents and at the start of most illnesses the doctor can be seen in the usual surgery hours.

In some cases a doctor must be seen **at once** either at home or at the hospital or surgery.

Here are some of them:

Long or repeated faints

All other kinds of unconsciousness

First or bad epileptic fits

Blood coughed up

Blood in bowel motions

Blood in urine

Sickness looking like coffee grounds

Bowels motions which look black and sticky

Sudden or continued bleeding "outside" body

Any loss of blood in pregnant women

Bad accidents

Any eye accidents

Severe shock or fright

Continued bad pain

High temperature, e.g. 104°F

Paralysis

Severe depression

Sudden bad sickness and diarrhoea

Loss of memory

All accidents to babies

Stings in the mouth

Snake bites

In the following cases the doctor should be telephoned or sent a message (before 10 a.m. if possible):

Rashes

Sore throats

Continued sickness or diarrhoea

Temperature of 100°F or over

Glands in neck swollen

Children's coughs ending in a whoop
Bad aching of head or limbs when polio is about
If several people start being sick
Any real sign of illness in babies or small children

Is somebody is sent to fetch a doctor it's better to write the message down—this is most important if children are sent.

e.g. What's happened
To how many people
Any special danger, e.g. heavy bleeding, no breathing, etc.

First Aid Box

Any box or small cupboard can be used as long as it will keep the things clean and dry.
Here are some of the things it should contain:

Bottles of Dettol or T.C.P.
Tube of Savlon
Roll of Elastoplast about 2 inches wide
Tin of waterproof adhesive dressing (mixed sizes)
Pair of clean scissors (round ends safer)
Pair of tweezers
Cotton wool
Lint
Safety pins, small and large
Eye bath
Crepe bandage 3 inches wide
Two triangular bandages
Three roller bandages, 1-inch, 2-inch and 3-inch
Wound dressings, large, medium and small
Small bowl, unbreakable
Packet of paper tissues
Roll of gauze
Anti-histamine ointment
Pair of real rubber gloves (ready powdered inside)
Gag in case of fits.
Graduated medicine glass. Thermometer (unless these are in your regular medicine cupboard).

Notes

1. Once a packet of cotton wool, gauze, etc., is opened, the rest should be wrapped up to keep it clean.
2. Don't run out of anything, buy some more before it gets used up.
3. Make it a rule that safety pins, scissors, etc., are not to be used for other purposes.
4. Close everything after use.
5. Know your kit! Any directions on bottles, packets, etc. should have been read **before** accidents occur, although it's still wise to read again for safety.
6. Make sure the doctor's telephone number is firmly fixed on the door or lid of the first aid box.

Medicine

How to Use Medicine Safely

All medicine should always be treated with great care. Used properly it cures people but used wrongly it can kill.

GIVING OR TAKING MEDICINE

People have got so used to medicine that they often forget how important it is to give it or take it correctly.

This is even more important these days because many more of the medicines used may be dangerous if not taken correctly.

Always be sure to give or take:

the RIGHT MEDICINE
in the RIGHT AMOUNT
at the RIGHT TIMES

General rules are:

1. Read **everything** on the label when you get it.
2. Check the amount before and after measuring **every** time.
3. Use a graduated medicine glass for liquids, don't use spoons.
4. Count pills, tablets, etc. very carefully.
5. Keep the label clean. (Pour from bottles with the label on top.)

Put a new one on if the other one gets dirty. Be careful to copy the dose, etc. correctly.

6. Put the medicine away in a safe place after every use. (Best to lock it up.)
7. If one dose has been missed, never give, or take, extra next time!

Notes

1. When giving tablets or capsules to children, never call them sweets. They will try to get more when you are not looking.
2. Don't take medicines in front of small children. They always want some of "what Mummy or Daddy has".
3. Never give anybody else your medicine.
4. Never take anybody else's medicine.
    If anybody does take the wrong medicine (or too much of their own):

    (*a*) If they are ill—get the doctor or take them to the hospital (Casualty department).
    (*b*) If they seem all right—it's still safer to let a doctor know.

5. Never take more than the label says.
    Never give anybody extra.
    Medicine is only safe if the right amount is taken, too much may be dangerous.
6. It's a good idea to make a quick note of how much medicine is left in the bottle, etc. after each dose. Then if you do leave it on the table by accident you can tell if any has gone.
7. Best if whoever takes the last dose mentions it.
8. Check quickly if you notice an empty aspirin or sleeping tablet container.
9. Pregnant women should never take **any** medicine (even for travelling) without asking the doctor first.

LOOKING AFTER MEDICINE

It should be somebody's job to see that there is a safe place to keep medicine and to keep a check on it.

It's best never to let small children see where you put medicine.

Some adults carry their tablets round with them to be on the safe side. Care must be taken, however, not to lose the tablets or leave handbags or jackets around where children are.

A few extra hints:

1. Don't keep old medicine. It's best to:

(*a*) Take it back to the chemist.

(*b*) Put it down the lavatory. (Undo capsules and squash tablets first or they may stay in the lavatory, then a child is sure to take them out.)

2. Never take medicine out of its proper container and put it in something else.

   Sometimes people need to take a few tablets to work. In this case it's safer to stick a label on the tin, etc., to say what the tablets are for, what the dose is, when they have to be taken and whose they are.

The medicine chest or cupboard

Whatever is used as a medicine chest MUST

1. Have a lock and key. Safer still if the door needs two hands to open it.
2. Be strong. (A small painted safe may be safer!)
3. Have no mirror so that the chest will not be used for cosmetics or shaving things.
4. Have two parts:

   (*a*) One for ordinary medicines taken by mouth.

   (*b*) The other for anything else.

   e.g. Anything marked POISON—This is often printed in very small letters, especially on tubes of ointment.
   Anything marked for EXTERNAL USE ONLY (for use outside the body).
   Anything for the ears, eyes, or nose.
   Anything you are not sure of.

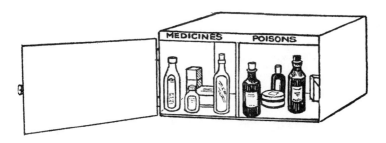

Note

Anything the chemist puts in brown bottles with ridges on is poisonous.

How to use the medicine cupboard

1. NEVER—Get medicines out in the dark—put the light on first.
2. NEVER—Let very sick people get their own medicine.
3. NEVER—Let small children get medicines out.
4. NEVER—Put animals' medicine in it. Put this in a SAFE place somewhere else.
5. NEVER—Use it for FIRST AID things or "Beauty" things.

ALWAYS

1. Lock the cupboard when you take medicines out.
2. Lock the cupboard when you put medicines back.
3. Keep the cupboard clean and tidy but don't put those "last few pills" into a box of different pills!

Where to put the medicine cupboard:

1. The medicine cupboard and the key must be put where:

   Grown-ups can get to them easily
   Small children can't get at them.

   This is not easy but must be done.
2. If it's kept in the bathroom, make sure you have a separate cupboard for toilet things. (The point against putting it in the bathroom is that children do spend time in there alone.)
3. Many homes find it safer to keep the medicine cupboard in the parents' room, but if a small child has to share the room another place might be safer.

Note

Don't forget to take as much care with medicines, etc., you don't get from the doctor, as those you do, e.g.

Medicines, skin creams, eye drops, etc., you buy from:

Chemists
Chain stores
Supermarkets
The "shop round the corner"
etc.

SPECIAL NOTES

1. Aspirin

This has become such an everyday remedy that people often keep it on the mantelpiece or a shelf in the kitchen or by the bed.

Always remember that ASPIRIN CAN KILL PEOPLE.

This can happen when:

(a) Babies are given grown-up aspirin.

(b) Small children get hold of the bottle and eat grown-up aspirins **or** junior aspirins.

(c) Anybody takes too many aspirins to get rid of very bad pain.

ASPIRINS SHOULD BE KEPT IN THE MEDICINE CUPBOARD.

DON'T KEEP GIVING ASPIRINS TO BABIES AND SMALL CHILDREN TO KEEP THEM QUIET.

And DON'T let children dose themselves with aspirin.

Remember

(a) Aspirin or tablets containing aspirin (acetyl salicylic acid) does not suit some people.

In this case it's safer to ask the doctor to recommend tablets which don't contain aspirin.

(b) Adults should not take more than six aspirins a day unless the doctor says so.

(c) Don't give aspirins to people:

If they have bad stomach pains (unless the doctor says so).

If they have been sick and brought up blood.

After an accident if they have been unconscious.

(d) NEVER give aspirins (even junior ones) to babies unless the doctor says so.

(e) Remember that aspirin poisoning does not cause a person to become quickly unconscious as for instance sleeping pills do.

First symptoms may be red face, sickness and blood, continual crying in babies, blood when the person goes to the lavatory, and thirst.

Treat for poisoning, i.e. Get the person to hospital at once.

(f) Aspirin is safe for most people when used properly.

2. Sleeping tablets

If the tablets are on the bedside table a person can easily forget they have taken them and take some more, which may kill them.

The best thing is

(a) To keep the tablets in the medicine cupboard.

(b) To take only the one dose into the bedroom.

NEVER give a grown-up's sleeping pill to small children.

3. Drugs for depression

Whether these are the "calming down" or "brightening up" kind, take extra care:

(*a*) To see nobody else takes them

(*b*) Not to take them before doing anything where you need normal control, e.g. driving, flying, risky jobs, etc. unless the doctor says so.

4. Very depressed people

If somebody in the family (or a visitor) is suffering from bad depression, it is everybody's duty to do anything they can to see that the person doesn't take an overdose of a dangerous drug, e.g.

(*a*) Don't leave big bottles of aspirin lying around.

(*b*) Don't leave any dangerous drugs about (the medicine cupboard may not be the safest place in this case).

(*c*) If you have any control over the person's drugs ordered by the doctor, don't leave them by the bedside or anywhere where the person can keep seeing them.

(*d*) A daily count of the pills is not a bad idea too.

Note

If anybody ever talks seriously, or several times jokingly, about committing suicide, get them to see a doctor.

But

1. Don't be too obvious about all this because it is so easy to **suggest** things to people.

2. If all reasonable care has been taken and an accident does happen, nobody need feel at fault.

5. Alcohol

A person may be killed if they drink alcohol around the time they are taking the following:

Large doses of Vitamin B
Some sleeping tablets
Some "calming down" drugs.

It is not a bad idea when the doctor is writing out the prescription to ask him if it's all right to take alcohol whilst taking the medicine. This should also be remembered by people who:

(*a*) Buy themselves Vitamin B tablets, etc.

(*b*) Take other people's drugs!

6. Food

It is important with some modern drugs not to eat certain foods.

The doctor will give the patient a card, telling him which food not to eat.

The person must:

(*a*) Read the card.
(*b*) Take care of it. (Carry it around.)
(*c*) Refer to it often.

This is another case where it is dangerous to take medicine prescribed for somebody else!

7. Mixing medicines

Medicines don't always "go together". It may be dangerous if you are already taking one kind of medicine from the doctor, or anywhere else, to start taking some other medicine at the same time. Safest to ask the doctor first.

Safety from Illness

 ## Safe Food

Food may

Look good
Smell good
Taste good

But if you eat it you may get illnesses such as:

Food poisoning
Typhoid
Paratyphoid fever
Tuberculosis
Dysentery
Gastro-enteritis.

This happens when the food contains **harmful bacteria.** How do the harmful bacteria get in the food?

They are carried there by:

People
Insects
Any dirt or filth getting on to food
The air—dust, moisture
Infected water
Animals.

People infect food by:

Touching it with unwashed hands after using the toilet.
Letting cuts or bandages on hands touch the food.
By touching pimples, sores, etc., and then touching food.
By touching the nose or mouth or ears and then touching food.
By coughing or sneezing on the food.

Which people infect food?

People who are just starting, have got, or are getting the above illnesses.
People who are quite better from some illnesses but still carry the germs.
People who feel perfectly WELL but themselves carry germs.

What can a mother do to make sure the food her family eats is safe?

She must be very careful about

Buying the food
Storing it
Preparing it
Serving it.

She must make sure

Everything that touches the food is clean
The kitchen is clean
Insects or mice don't get on it

This looks unpleasant *and* it's dangerous

Dangerous *and* disgusting

Dust and dirt don't get on it
The rubbish bin is emptied often.

Buying

1. Use a clean shopping bag.
2. Buy from clean shops.
3. Buy from shops where customers can't cough or sneeze over easily infected food.
4. Only accept food wrapped in clean paper.
5. Buy from shops where the assistants are clean, e.g.
   They don't do these kinds of things whilst serving—

   Scratch heads
   Touch noses (or worse)
   Wear dirty bandages on hands, or have uncovered cuts
   Lick their fingers
   Blow in bags to open them
   Use their hands to pick up bacon, cakes, etc.

6. When buying cooked meats from butcher's or butchery counters, never buy the cooked meat if the same assistant is

serving cooked and raw meat. They are not allowed to do this, but it sometimes happens.

7. Don't buy frozen food from shops where fridges are over-flowing or frozen food is kept out of fridges.

Make sure the food is rock hard when you buy it.

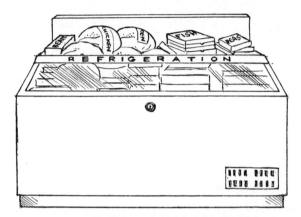

Food is not safe in an overflowing cabinet

8. Mind where you put the shopping bag.
9. Be clean in shops yourself, e.g. no touching food, sneezing over food, breathing over food or taking dogs in!
10. Buy from shops where cooked meat foods are kept in a chill cabinet.

What can you do if the nicest assistant has the nastiest habit? A quiet word when the shop is empty will probably do the trick.

If there's only one shop and asking nicely doesn't help? The Public Health Department will!

Bad food or food with bits of wood, glass, etc. in must always be reported to the Public Health Department. Keep the food to show them.

Eating out

It's safer to take your own food if you can't find a café where

The premises are clean

The assistants are clean

The plates, cups, etc. are clean and not chipped.

Storing and keeping food

Easily infected foods (see p. 181) should be kept:

(*a*) For the shortest time possible
(*b*) Cold (in a fridge if possible)
(*c*) Protected from damp air.

1. Put all perishable foods straight into a clean fridge.
2. Keep all food cold, clean, and covered in a dry place. Make sure covers are spotless!
3. Frozen foods:

   (*a*) Don't keep them longer than it says on the packet.
   (*b*) Don't take them out of the fridge, let them thaw, and then put them back in. Bacteria multiply very quickly and make the food dangerous even if refrozen.
4. Never put food which you think might be a bit "off" in the fridge. It will still be dangerous and will infect other food.
   Don't fill the fridge too full. Air must be able to circulate.
6. If you haven't a fridge:

   (*a*) Put perishable food in a clean cold larder, on a marble slab if possible.
   (*b*) Don't put food on the larder floor.
   (*c*) Cover the food to keep flies, etc., off.

Food protected from insects

   (*d*) Always use really clean containers and lids.
   (*e*) Make sure it's still fresh before using it.
   See also p. 182.

7. Use up all perishable foods as soon as you can.
8. Never put pet food near human food.
   If you put pet food in the fridge, bacteria from it can get into the human food (without the foods actually touching) and the whole family can be poisoned.
9. Always use first the food which has been stored longest.

PET FOOD?
NO!

10. Don't store anything but food in fridges or larders.
11. Keep fridges and larders very clean.

Preparing and serving food

1. Wash hands before handling food. Be extra careful if the food is ready to eat, e.g. cold meat, etc.
2. Wash hands, chopping board and knife after chopping raw meat.
3. Wash hands after using toilet—this is MOST IMPORTANT.
4. Keep finger nails short and very clean. Take extra care if you use nail varnish. Ideally varnish shouldn't be worn when preparing food!
4. Wear a clean apron and don't let hair hang all over food.
5. Never smoke while preparing food.
6. Never put the spoon used for tasting back into the food.
7. If there's nobody else to get the food ready, take extra care if:

   (a) You have a cold—Use paper handkerchiefs, once only, and then put them in the fire or down the lavatory.
   (b) If you have to blow your nose or touch your hanky, best to wash hands afterwards.
   (c) Never cough or sneeze on to your hand.
   (d) If you have a cut, boil, scratch, etc., cover it with a water-proof dressing.

8. Try not to touch food more than is necessary.
9. Serve hot foods as soon as possible after they are ready.

This isn't the moment to smoke

Make sure that anybody who helps or comes near the food keeps these rules too.

Notes

1. Preparing in advance, e.g. meat, meat puddings and pies.
   This often has to be done to save time, but always:

   (*a*) Cool the food quickly. Cut a piece out of puddings and pies. (Put it back when cool.) Protect the food from flies whilst cooling but don't seal tightly.

   (*b*) Put the cool food in the fridge. Hot food can be cooled quickly in the fridge if there is no other food in there to spoil.

   (*c*) Don't part cook joints one day and finish cooking the next, it can be dangerous.

2. Left overs:

   (*a*) Try not to have any.

   (*b*) Don't leave oddments too long in the fridge.

(c) It's safer never to keep gravy, custard, jellies, even in the fridge. Bacteria multiply very quickly in these.

3. Reheated foods (left-overs or bought pies, etc.)

(a) Just warming or making really hot for only a few minutes multiplies germs.

(b) Recommended oven time is 20 minutes at Gas regulo 7, Electric 425°F (after the oven is hot).
On top of the stove—bring to the boil and then cook for at least 15 minutes.

Most easily infected foods

It is as well to know which these are and to take extra care of them.

1. All cold cooked meat and dishes containing meat, e.g. sausages, brawn, stews, pies, sausage rolls. Also gravy, soups, and made sauces.
Never serve underdone pork.
2. Any food with gelatine in it, e.g. jellies, trifles, pies, etc.
3. Custard, ice cream, synthetic cream, fresh cream cakes.
4. Shell fish.
5. Watercress and salad foods. (Wash very carefully.)
6. Eggs, especially duck eggs. (It's safer not to use them raw or underdone.) Cook duck eggs at least 10 minutes.
7. Sandwiches—meat, fish, egg, pastes.

It is important that special care is taken in the buying, preparation storing and cooking where necessary of all these foods.

EXTRA REMINDERS

1. **Pork and hams** should never be underdone.
2. Never let children eat **raw pork sausages** or sausage meat— they can become very ill. Sausages need to be fried slowly after first few minutes so that the insides are properly cooked.
3. **Powdered and dried foods** must be eaten as soon as possible after they have been made up. If this is impossible, they must be stored in the fridge.
4. **Canned foods**—don't use them if they don't smell or look good. Wipe tops before opening. Never use food from tins if the ends bulge. Take care with home bottled foods too.
5. **Animal food**—raw pet meat is always a possible source of food poisoning for the family, unless it is sterilised before being sold. Separate knives, plates, etc. must be used and these must be washed separately and the sink cleaned afterwards.

If animals only have human food, they must not be allowed to clean up the family's plates and dishes too!

6. Dangerous times—food poisoning is more likely to occur

(*a*) In summer months

(*b*) At Christmas and party times

(*c*) When somebody in the family is ill with such things as intestinal illnesses, sore throats, etc.

Be careful to give them their own towel, crockery, etc., and wash these things separately too.

7. Some food poisoning symptoms are:

(*a*) Abdominal pains

(*b*) Sickness

(*c*) Diarrhoea

(*d*) High temperature

(*e*) Giddiness.

Diarrhoea in babies, especially in summer, should be taken seriously and the doctor called.

If anybody is taken ill in this way, don't forget to keep any remains of the suspected food for examination.

If several members of the family get the above symptoms at the same time, call the doctor at once.

8. Babies' food (see also p. 110)

Clinics, health visitors and midwives will give precise instructions on how to prepare babies' food safely and keep bottles, etc. safe. Their instructions must be followed exactly because:

(*a*) Harmful bacteria grow very easily and quickly in milk.

(*b*) Babies can quickly get very ill with gastro-enteritis and other milk-carried illnesses.

9. Keeping food safe without a fridge

The aim is still to keep the food

Cold, clean, covered

Not wetter than it is naturally.

Helpful equipment—

(*a*) Butter and milk coolers. One type is made of terra-cotta. The milk cooler has to be soaked in cold water for about ten minutes. It will keep milk cool for about 24 hours.

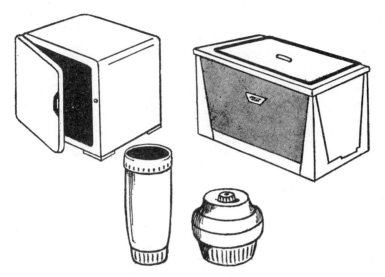

Two cooling cabinets, a milk cooler and a butter cooler

The butter cooler has a glass lining. The outside has to be soaked for about ten minutes in cold water.

(*b*) Cooling cabinets.

One type has a tank at the bottom which has to be filled with water. The cabinet soaks up the water which keeps the cabinet and the food cool. Another type has no water tank. The cabinet itself has to be soaked with water.

(*c*) A box made of polystyrene. It keeps cold food cold for about 24 hours. It is meant for picnics but can be very useful for storing milk, butter, etc.

(*d*) Polythene canisters will keep out moisture, dust and insects, but don't put meat in them.

(*e*) Large clean vacuum flasks are useful for keeping all kinds of cold food cold or hot food hot. (Don't leave hot food in for too long.)

(*f*) Nylon net covers for all kinds of food.

(*g*) Any kind of basin and a piece of butter muslin can be used to keep milk cool.

Put the bottle of milk in a basin. Fill the basin with water. Put wet butter muslin over the bottle so that the ends dip in the water. Change the water every so often. (Illustration overleaf.)

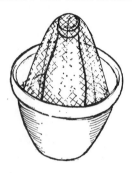

Notes

1. If you haven't a fridge, it's safer to eat perishable foods the same day as you buy them, especially meat pies and cooked meats.
2. Don't buy too much at once.

Serving

1. Serve prepared food as soon as possible.
2. Be extra careful with party food. Keep meats, jellies, and custard in the fridge or in a cool place as long as possible.
3. Clear food from table as soon as meal is finished.

Washing up

1. Scrape and rinse plates, pans, etc., before washing up.
2. Use hot water and some kind of washing up liquid.
3. Change water when dirty.
4. Rinse under hot water and put to drain rather than dry on towels.
5. If you do use tea towels, don't let people use them to dry hands on.
6. Wear gloves if you have a cut or any skin trouble, or if detergent makes hands rough or cracked.
7. Keep all cloths, mops, scourers, etc. very clean.

When handling clean things:

(a) Cups, dishes, bowls, jugs, etc. try not to put your hands inside.

(b) Cutlery—only hold the handles.

Try not to use:

Chipped or cracked cups
Spoons and forks if the top metal has worn off. Germs adhere to rough surfaces and in cracks.

THE KITCHEN

A really clean kitchen is essential if food is to be kept clean and safe.

Regular cleaning is very important and everything should be done to make this as easy and effective as possible.

Floors

Whatever the floor is made of, or covered with, should give a smooth surface and be easily cleaned.

Cracks, poor joins, holes and rough surfaces collect dirt and germs.
Vinyl, good lino, well fitted tiles are all suitable.

Walls

Should be smooth and washable.
Rounded corners make cleaning easier.
Tiles, gloss paint and vinyl are all easily cleaned.

Ceilings

The important things are:

(*a*) There should be no loose bits to fall into food.
(*b*) That moisture should not collect and fall into food. This means any covering must be absorbent.

Paper and paint are not suitable for ceilings if moisture can collect and condense on them.

Non-washable distemper is good but really needs to be re-done about every 6 months.

Lighting

Good lighting is very important for cleanliness

(*a*) So that dirt can be noticed, especially in corners, etc.
(*b*) Because many insects like dark corners.

Ventilation

Bacteria multiply very quickly in warm steamy places. To cut down this danger it is important to have a current of air to:
Cool the kitchen
Take out steam and fumes.

Kitchen windows should always be open at least a little when cooking is being done.

In areas where there are a lot of insects and in basement kitchens where a lot of dust flies in, it is best to fix fine gauze wire over the windows. This must be kept very clean, of course.

Extra helps to ventilation are:

Extractor fans
Canopies with extractor fans to fit over cookers.

Lavatories

Should never open into kitchens but they often do.

The only thing to do is to keep the lavatory, sink, and kitchen very clean and be very strict about the hand washing rule for all the family.

Equipment

All the equipment in kitchens should be:

(a) Easy to clean
(b) Easy to undo and put together again. (If it is awkward, it won't get cleaned often!)
(c) It is very important to wash white and shiny things really well. They look so clean with just a wipe that the danger of germs gets overlooked!

Sinks

Old rough sinks collect germs, but if there is no hope of a new one extra care has to be taken, e.g.

Plenty of rinsing with hot water
The use of bleach for cleaning
Keeping it as free from grease as possible.

Ideally sinks which are used for washing dishes, cutlery and other things connected with food, shouldn't be used for hand washing, floor mop rinsing, etc.!

A double sink helps here, but if this isn't possible use a separate bowl for washing up.

Cupboards and shelves, tables, etc.

These are more hygienic if they have hard smooth surfaces.

Metal and glass and Formica are better than wood. Wooden shelves should be covered with a washable material or given two or three coats of gloss paint.

The fewer ledges, corners, and joins there are the better.

Floor standing equipment should:

(a) Have legs long enough to make cleaning under it easy, or be nearly flat on the floor.
(b) Be easy to pull out to clean behind.

The rest of the equipment

Everything to do with food and the kitchen should be:

(*a*) Bought with an eye to easy and complete cleaning.
(*b*) Be kept very clean at all times.
(*c*) When utensils become chipped or difficult to clean, throw them away, if possible.

Cleaning

Making things look clean is never enough when the things are connected with food.

Danger spots are:

1. Table tops, etc.—never doing any more than just wiping them is not enough. They need a proper hot water wash at least once a day.
2. Slots in sliding cupboard doors collect dirt and bits of food.
3. The little ledge on the top of half tiled walls holds dirt and grease, especially behind equipment.
4. The cupboard under the sink and pipes.
5. Plug holes of sinks, overflow outlets and behind taps.
6. The cutlery drawer.
7. The outside drain—needs a boiling soda water wash at least once a week. Take the grid out to clean it if possible.
8. Pedal bins and dustbins need hot water scrubs and disinfectant. Pedal bins should be emptied, washed and clean paper put in at least daily. Always keep the lids on bins and wrap rubbish in paper.
9. Larders—the floor, underneath of shelves, walls, any air bricks, doors, and wire gauze at window all need regular cleaning.
10. The part of the yard leading up to the back door, if this leads into the kitchen, must be kept clean. Bits of food dropped on the way to the dustbin will attract rats and mice as well as insects.
11. Using tea towels for drying hands on and wiping up spills spreads germs. So does wiping the floor with the dish cloth!
   It is safer to use all cloths for their proper purpose. Use paper kitchen rolls if possible for mopping up jobs.

PESTS

As has already been said, insects, mice and rats all spread disease.

One way of attracting rats and mice

Rats and mice

To prevent these coming into the house:

1. Never leave scraps of food about anywhere.
2. Always put food away, especially at night.
3. Fill up any holes in the floor or walls.
4. Keep drains in good repair.
5. Keep lids on dustbins.
6. Put only small pieces of food out for birds. Large pieces attract rats!

Some of the signs that rats and mice are getting into the house are:

Holes they have made
Droppings
Greasy marks along the bottom of walls
Small teeth marks on food.

To get rid of them

1. Take extra care to keep food covered and shut up.
2. Try traps and cheese for mice. If this doesn't work and you get something poisonous—

   (a) Lock it up somewhere outside the house.
   (b) Take great care to see children don't touch it or eat it.

(c) Be careful pets don't get near the bait.
(d) Scrub hands and nails if you touch poison.
(e) Don't touch dead rats or mice with your hands.
(f) Don't let poison touch food, tables or utensils.
(g) Follow directions exactly.
(h) If anybody feels sick or ill when poison has been used for pests make sure they see a doctor.
(i) Remove every trace of poison when finished with.

3. If you suspect even one rat it's best to tell the Public Health Department and let them deal with it.

Insects

These include flies, wasps, cockroaches, ants, beetles, etc.
As it's impossible to keep food covered every minute of the day something has to be done to kill insects.
Whatever you buy:

(a) Read and follow the directions exactly.
(b) Keep the stuff away from children.
(c) If you use a spray, make sure all food has been put away first. Safer to wash table tops, etc., afterwards.

Hygiene

It is often said that "prevention is better than cure". This is very true regarding illness.
Good hygiene goes a very long way to prevent illness.
Children should be taught, and all the family should practise good health habits.

HEALTHY HABITS

1. A daily wash all over—a bath is better still.
2. Daily teeth cleaning—at least at night.
3. Regular hair washing.
4. Keeping nails short and clean—"clean" is the important word.
5. Always using a handkerchief—no sniffing.

Now wash your hands!

6. Not straining eyes

    (*a*) Reading in a poor light, e.g. under the bedclothes.
    (*b*) Working with a bright light in front of you.

7. Looking after feet

    (*a*) Putting them up when possible.
    (*b*) Soaking them when they ache.
    (*c*) Always wearing well fitting shoes.

8. Standing, sitting and walking correctly—not too much slouching and lolling.

    But—tired people, especially children, can't help slouching.

9. Getting enough:

sleep
fresh air
exercise in the fresh air
sunshine

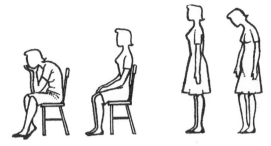

Straight, not droopy is better for you and looks nicer too

Sunshine and fresh air are your friends

10. Wearing clothes which are

    (*a*) Clean
    (*b*) Warm in winter and cool in summer
    (*c*) Not too tight or uncomfortably loose.

For many reasons it isn't always possible to keep these habits regularly. When this is the case, people have to do the best they can, e.g.

If a good night's sleep is not possible:

    (*a*) Try to get at least one 10 minute nap in the daytime.
    (*b*) Sit for as many jobs as possible.

When hot water is short:

    (*a*) Stick to the handwashing rules at least, even if it has to be cold water sometimes.

(*b*) Wash the body a bit each day, get an all-over wash as often as possible.

A rub all over with a towel is better than nothing.

(*c*) Use public baths if there are some near.

(*d*) Make the most of hot water and any showers at work and school.

(*e*) Comb or brush the hair several times a day. Use a dry shampoo if available.

(*f*) Clothes

Underclothes—try to wash these regularly.

Top clothes —Try not to get them too dirty. Brush and shake, then hang them in the fresh air if possible.

Hang clothes at night rather than fold them or leave them in a heap.

When toothpaste is short:

(*a*) A brisk brushing with water alone is good.

(*b*) Rinsing the mouth with clean water helps too.

When fresh air is short:

(*a*) Remember early morning air is the freshest in cities. Try to walk part way to work.

(*b*) Make the most of any parks or recreation grounds.

(*c*) Try to get out for days or half days to places where the air is fresher.

(*d*) Practise breathing deeply when you do get into fresh air.

(*e*) Keep out of smoky and foggy atmospheres as much as possible.

A CLEAN HOME

A clean home is vital for the health of all the family. Everything should be done:

(*a*) To prevent the home getting dirty

(*b*) To get rid of dirt and dust.

To prevent the home getting dirty:

(*a*) Use surfaces and materials to which dirt and dust don't cling easily, e.g.

Metal, glass, Formica, etc.
Fibreglass for curtains
Plastic furniture coverings
Vinyl flooring (but remember this can be very slippery)
Hard gloss paints
    etc.

Things which are hard and shiny and don't scratch or become rough, keep cleaner than soft, absorbent, easily scratched things.

(*b*) Don't keep a lot of things which are never used but only collect dust.

(*c*) Try not to have rooms so full of things that it's hard to get round to clean up.

(*d*) Train everybody to be as clean as possible in the home, e.g.

Changing into slippers as they come in
Cleaning up spills at once
Giving help with the general cleaning.

To get rid of dirt and dust:

(*a*) Try to get as much cleaning equipment and materials as possible which will

Clean properly
Do their job as quickly and easily as possible.

But, don't use cleaners which are too harsh for the job and so make surfaces rough.

(*b*) Take care of equipment.

Don't waste cleaning materials if you know you will have to go without until you have money to buy more.

(*c*) Make sure all the rooms get a good clean in turn.

(*d*) Have a daily cleaning plan.

General hints

1. Keep the home as well aired as possible.
2. Make sure beds get aired regularly (but don't air them for hours on a wet day with the window wide open!).
3. Don't let rubbish collect anywhere.
4. "Little and often" cleaning is better than letting dirt and germs collect.
5. Damp cloths and cloths with a little polish on, and mops too, are often more effective than dry dusters and brushes and brooms.
6. Keep all cleaning equipment clean. Empty vacuum cleaners and sweepers regularly.
7. Try to keep floors extra clean if there is a baby at crawling stage.
8. Keep the lavatory very clean but

   (*a*) Remind family to flush lavatory before using it if they see lavatory powder still in it.

   (*b*) Only use bleach when everybody is out. It will do its job in about half an hour. Don't leave it in all night, the first person who uses the lavatory in the morning may get splashed with it.

9. Train everybody to wash baths and washbasins after they have used them.
10. Keep all towels and flannels clean. If possible, give everybody their own.
11. Don't let dust collect on tops of doors, pelmets, wardrobes and other high places.

HEALTHY EATING

What we eat plays a very important part in keeping us safe from illness.

Here is a simple daily plan for most people.

1. 1 pint milk—more if you like.
2. Meat or fish for dinner.
3. 1 oz. cheese for breakfast or tea.

4. 1 egg for breakfast or tea.
5. Some green vegetables, cooked or raw.
6. Some fruit with Vitamin C in it, e.g. oranges, grapefruit, blackcurrants, strawberries.
7. Cod liver oil or halibut oil if prescribed.
8. Bread and butter, jam, etc., potatoes.
9. Plenty of water.

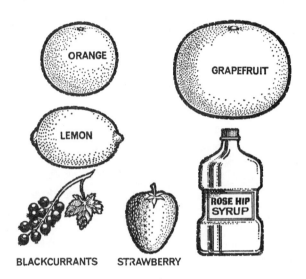

Some foods with good Vitamin C content

These should be included once or twice a week (more often if you like)

Liver
Herrings
Carrots
Bacon

Extra meat, milk, fish, eggs, cheese are good for most people, if they can get them.

When it's hard to get all these things for the family every day:

1. Make sure children eat their school dinner if they have it.
   Get them to buy oranges instead of sweets if they have any pocket money.

2. Remember mothers must have their share of the foods above. They must eat or drink any welfare foods they are entitled to, not let the family have them.

3. Train the family to eat raw shredded greens and grated carrot.

4. Don't waste food:

> (a) When preparing it, e.g. don't throw away dark green leaves, put them in the pan first so that they cook longer.
>
> (b) By not cooking it properly.
>
> (c) By letting children leave it.

5. Try to buy any cheap foods the clinic may sell.

Planning menus

1. Put some protein food in each meal, e.g.

Breakfast—Egg
Elevenses—Milk
Dinner—Meat or fish
High Tea—Cheese
Supper—Milk

2. Put in some vegetables, raw, cooked or some of each, e.g.

Dinner—Cabbage
Tea—Raw green vegetables in salad

3. Add some Vitamin C fruit where you like, e.g.

Oranges	Blackcurrants
Grapefruit	Strawberries

4. Add the starch and sugar foods, e.g.

Bread	Pudding
Potatoes	Cakes
Cereals	Jam

Then:

1. Check every day's menus for

Milk
Greens
Fruit with Vitamin C in it.

2. Check every week's menus for

Liver
Herrings
Other fish

Carrots
Bacon

What's in what

1. These foods "keep you going"—they are "**energy** foods".

STARCH AND SUGAR	FAT	VITAMIN B
Bread	Butter	Pork, bacon, ham
Foods made with flour	Margarine	Food with yeast in
	Fat in food	Liver, kidney, heart
Sugar	Fat food is cooked in	Bread
Foods made with sugar		Cod's roe
Cereals		Eggs
Potatoes		

(a) Use some as they are.
(b) Put others together, e.g.

Bacon and beans
Fried cod's roe and chips
Bacon roll, steamed or baked
Pork pies
Ham sandwiches
etc.

Warning

Eating too many starchy and sugary foods makes people too fat. Many children are too fat nowadays.

But

If you don't eat enough you may get too tired.

2. Foods for healthy **nerves** and **skin**.

Milk	Meat
Yeast foods	Fish
Liver and kidney	Eggs
Cod's roe	

Serve them like this:

Bacon and eggs
Liver and bacon
Put yeast in buns and cakes instead of baking powder
etc.

3. Foods for **strong bones** and **teeth**.

Milk	Oranges
Cheese	Grapefruit
Sardines plus bones	Blackcurrants
Salmon plus bones	Strawberries
Bread	Greens
plus cod liver oil and sunshine	

Use them like this:

Milk puddings
Milk shakes
Cheese and potato pie
Welsh rarebit
Cheese and raw greens in salad
Grapefruit for breakfast
Blackcurrant tart
Fresh orange juice

4. Foods for **growth** and for **repairing** the body.

Milk	Cereals
Meat	Pulses (peas, beans, lentils)
Fish	Nuts
Eggs	
Cheese	

Use them like this:

Bacon and beans
Meat and vegetable pie
Baked beans or peas added to shepherd's pie
Macaroni cheese
Spaghetti with cheese or meat
Curried meat and rice
Meat pies and puddings
Rice puddings and milk moulds
Bread and butter pudding
Milk with breakfast cereals
Sweet corn with poached egg

5. Foods for **good rich blood**.

Liver	Dried fruit
Eggs	Black treacle
Watercress	Chocolate
Greens	

Use them like this:

Treacle in gingerbread instead of syrup
Liver and onions
Liver sausage sandwiches
Liver and bacon
Chocolate cakes and puddings
Scotch eggs

Note

A good mixed diet will usually supply most people with what they need.
If you think you need extra vitamins, it's best to see the doctor about it.

 # Avoidable Illnesses

Some illnesses are unavoidable but there are many which people need not get if they take care in time.
For instance, children need never get:

Smallpox
Diphtheria
Tetanus
Whooping cough
"Polio"
T.B.

Children can be kept safe from all these illnesses these days by immunization.
The Clinic or family doctor will tell parents the best time and how often to take their children to be done.
There are many illnesses which adults need not get or need not get badly if they take care in time.
It is up to everybody to take advantage of every health safeguard they can, e.g.

X rays
Cervical smear tests
"Check ups" and tests

Tetanus injections (if they work on the land or do a lot of gardening)
Ante-natal clinics

It is also up to everybody if they don't feel well:

(a) To go to the doctor
(b) To do what he says
(c) Not to spread infectious illnesses round the family (or to anybody else).

Addictions

These are better not begun because they are all difficult to stop. They can all make people very ill, e.g.

Smoking
Drinking
Taking drugs
Over-eating.

Young people should

(a) Have the dangers of these things sensibly pointed out to them before they are likely to meet up with them.
    Parents must take trouble to "keep up with things" so that they know danger points.
(b) Never be encouraged by older people to start doing them.
(c) Be told where to go for help if they do get entangled.

Over-eating is not often called an "addiction" but to many people it is and they would love to stop over-eating but can't.
As many illnesses can be caused by over-eating, it is important:

(a) That children should not be encouraged to over-eat.
(b) That advice should be sought from an understanding doctor or a psychiatrist before it's too late.

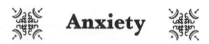 **Anxiety**

Some anxiety is useful for making people more careful or to do their best, etc., but when people get over-anxious they become unable to enjoy life or do their best at anything.
Some things which cause people too much anxiety are—children, money, jobs, health, getting old.

Some helps are:

1. Children

No parents can do more than—
(a) Train their children in the best ways they can.
(b) Get all the help they can in training their children.

2. Money

Money will be less of an anxiety if people—
(a) Budget carefully.
(b) Don't overdo H.P.
(c) Save what they can
(d) Take out what insurances they can
(e) Teach children how to manage money.

3. Jobs

Younger people have the chance, these days—
(a) To get the best qualifications they can
(b) To get into the right job for them
(c) To have a "second string", i.e. opportunities to earn extra money at some hobby or leisure time job.

There are more opportunities for older people to train for a new job these days too.

4. Health

Will be less of an anxiety if people—
(a) Keep the general health rules regarding sleep, exercise, fresh air, food, etc.
(b) Take advantage of all the modern positive health measures.
(c) Use leisure time well.
(d) Keep faith in doctors.

5. Retirement

Some secrets of a happy retirement are—
(a) Preparing long before it happens, e.g. if you are longing to retire to a certain little village, take regular holidays there beforehand to get to know the people, etc.
(b) Making as much provision as you can beforehand, e.g. insurance, somewhere to live, something to do, someone to share it with, etc.
(c) Not wearing yourself out during the few years before retirement, so that retirement becomes just a period of ill health.

(d) "Keeping your friendships in repair" before you retire. If you are too busy for people before retirement, people will be too busy for you after you retire.

(e) Remembering retirement only means retiring from tiring work, not from life or from the less tiring work.

6. Loneliness

Is the reason for constant anxiety among many people.

For many people it can be lessened by joining up with people with the same interests.

It can never be lessened by constantly longing for somebody who has died or gone for good.

It can never be lessened by staying indoors and being miserable.

A good trick is to sit down and think "What would I advise other people to do if they were lonely?", and go and do it yourself!

It is very important that people should:

(a) Bring up children to make friends
(b) Keep up with their own friends
(c) Keep their circle of family and friends open to newcomers
(d) "Keep the family together" (but **not** isolated).

7. Philosophy and Faith

Both these can keep people safe from anxiety but (a) they both need time set aside for thinking and (b) they both need to be hung on to like grim death in times of stress.

Where to get help

All the following and many others will help in times of anxiety:

Good families
Good friends
Citizens' Advice Bureaux
Doctors
Psychiatrists
Clergymen
Solicitors
Groups such as Divorced Women's groups or Cruse Clubs.

When it seems there is no help at hand the Samaritan organizations will help AT ONCE. It is a good idea to find out if there is a branch of this organization or other organizations, e.g. Leagues of Friendship, in your area **before** you need them.

Find out their telephone numbers because this is often the quickest method of contact. (Ask telephone operator if necessary.)

Outdoors

 **Road Safety**

Learning and practising road safety rules is a matter of life and death for everybody.

Road accidents can only be kept to a minimum if everybody regards road safety as a two-fold job:

(*a*) To keep oneself safe
(*b*) To keep others safe

As more and more traffic uses the roads, more and more rules have to be made.

It is therefore necessary that everybody should:

(*a*) Learn the basic rules of road safety
(*b*) Learn new rules as they are made.

WALKING

Small children

See p. 120 for general rules for keeping small children safe outdoors.

Older children

Whereas it is usually enough for the under fives to be taught only

basic road safety rules, e.g. "how to cross" and "not to play in the road", older children need to learn ALL the safety rules for "Road Users on Foot".

Although they are taught a lot at school, much teaching must be done outside school because this is when they are actually using the roads.

To keep the "over fives" safe—

1. They need continual teaching—they forget quickly.
2. They need continual example—by all adults!
3. They are still the responsibility of all road users.

General rules for keeping "over fives" safe on the roads are:

1. Parents (and the children when old enough) should possess a copy of the Highway Code.

   The rules for "The Road User on Foot" must be learnt and practised. Children could be tested:

   (*a*) On their knowledge of the rules
   (*b*) On how they practise the rules when they are out.

It is surprising how many people think the Highway Code is only for drivers!

2. Every area has its particular road danger spots.
   It is important:

   (*a*) That these black spots are pointed out to children.
   (*b*) That children are taught what to do at black spots.

3. It cannot be taught too often that

Zebra crossings are **not** MAGIC safety paths.

4. Teach them to read Road Safety words as soon as possible, e.g. "CROSS NOW", WAIT", "STOP", etc.

If you practise at home, use the same kind of letters that the words are written in on the traffic lights, etc.

Other rules to teach are:

1. Even if a driver waves you across it is still up to each person to CHECK FOR HIMSELF that the road is safe to cross.
2. Never hang on backs of lorries.
3. Never play at running across the roads in front of cars.

   (*a*) You may trip.
   (*b*) Cars often can't stop in time.

4. Never wander in the roads in busy shopping streets.

5. Walking at night:

   (*a*) Face oncoming traffic
   (*b*) It's safer to wear something white and to carry a torch. (Keep a look out for other safety wear too).

Note

As children get older, they can read the rest of the Highway Code. It is better still if "Road safety on foot" can be explained from the driver's point of view too.

General hints

1. Pushing prams

   (*a*) DON'T push it into the road and hope all the motorists will stop—they may not be able to.
   (*b*) DON'T let toddlers push the pram or pushchair unless you keep one hand on it yourself so that you can stop it at the kerb.
   (*c*) DO use crossings so that you can walk across. Having to rush suddenly with an unwieldy pram is too likely to result in an accident.
   (*d*) DO make sure the brake is on when you leave the pram AND make sure the pram is facing in a safe direction if the brake should fail.
   (*e*) NEVER wheel a pram from behind or in front of a parked vehicle, unless you absolutely must.

2. One-way streets

   (*a*) It's always wise to take a glance in the direction in which traffic should **not** come because now and again a car does go the wrong way.
   (*b*) Be extra careful when crossing at lights. From some directions it is impossible for the walker to even **see** the lights!

3. Always remember that not all drivers obey all the safe driving rules. Take care of **yourself**.
4. NEVER take any risks when crossing the roads with small children or old people. Remember they cannot run as quickly as you can.
5. In a hurry?

   Remember the policeman's warning, "It's better to be 10 minutes late in this world than 20 years too early in the next"!

6. Teach the children not to walk several abreast on the pavement so that other people have to step into the road.

Don't force other people into the road

7. It is safer never to try to cross the road in front of or behind a parked car, but if you must, be very careful.

Keep a lookout for other parked cars coming out as well as traffic already in the road.

CYCLING

Safe cycling starts with a safe machine. Although children often like looking after their own cycles it is up to parents to check them regularly for safety.

All children should be encouraged to take any cycling tests available.

General cycling rules are:

1. Know and practise the Highway Code.
2. Always ride in a way which is SAFE for yourself, SAFE for others, e.g. in single file.

Many cyclists **cause** accidents to other people, e.g. car drivers, without being actually in the accident themselves.

Never fool around or show off on a cycle even if the road seems empty.

3. Make sure anything you carry:

   (a) Is firmly fixed to the bicycle
   (b) Does not get in the way of your movements
   (c) Cannot get in the way of the movement of any part of the cycle
   (d) Does not stick out.

4. Don't overload your bicycle so that it is difficult to manage.
5. Don't ride more than two abreast even for a few minutes.
6. Toddlers—keep a lookout for them—they often run into the road suddenly.
7. Old people—take extra care—remember they often can't see, hear, or move very well even though they look all right.
8. Make sure you have your name and address and telephone number on you and on your cycle (in saddlebag perhaps) in case of accident.
9. If you have glasses, make sure you wear them when cycling.
10. Don't wear sun-glasses which are too dark or with wide side pieces. Both these things will stop you seeing properly.
11. Dress safely. Loose clothes and sloppy shoes can cause accidents.

Don't forget that you are more likely to have an accident if you are:

Very tired
Bad tempered
Not well

Note

It is up to the parents to see that:

(a) A child's bicycle is the right size and correctly adjusted to the child.
(b) Very young children don't ride in the road.
(c) The child knows and practises the road safety rules.

PUBLIC TRANSPORT

General safety rules are:

1. Never try to get on or off moving buses or trains.
2. Never try to get a bus to stop by standing in front of it.
3. Give the proper signal at request stops, i.e. remain standing on the pavement and put your arm out.
4. Never cross in front of or behind a stationary bus. Wait for the bus to move off.

5. Don't stand too near the edge of the pavement in bus queues.
6. Don't stand on the edge of the bus platform, you may be thrown off, especially when the bus goes round corners.
7. Don't stand too near the edge of station platforms—you may get pushed over the edge or knocked by opening doors.
8. Don't open train doors until the train has stopped.
9. Never hang out of train windows, you may get hit by a passing train (going the other way) or by a tunnel wall.
10. Don't lean on train doors.
11. Don't hang around at the top or bottom of stairs or escalators.
12. Don't push or fool around on or near buses or trains.

DRIVING

The first thing necessary for safe driving is a SAFE CAR.

As there is no list of which makes of car are safer than others it is up to everybody before they buy a car to:

(a) Decide what they want the car for, e.g. speed, children, etc.
(b) Collect as much information as possible to find out which car would be safest for the purpose.
(c) Make a list of all the extras which can be bought to make a car safer.
(d) Work out the price of the safest car for the required purpose. Can't afford it? The safest thing to do is to wait until you can.

Even the safest cars need proper MAINTENANCE:

Regular servicing and checking by experts
Everyday care by owners.

The Highway Code lays down rules for the safe condition necessary for all vehicles before being driven on the roads.

The safest thing is to do a quick safety drill before you drive long distances or at least once a week, e.g.

Tyres	Mirror	
Brakes	Windows	Doors
Steering	Seat	
Lights	Horn	Bonnet
Engine		

THE DRIVER

To drive safely a driver must be able to

CONTROL himself
CONTROL the car

To be able to do these things he must be in good condition himself.
People cannot drive safely if they are:

Drunk
Drugged
Tired
Unable to see properly
"Day dreaming"
In a bad temper
Showing off
Very upset
Very depressed
In too much of a hurry
  etc.

To prevent accidents:

1. Don't drink at all if you are going to drive.
   If you have been drinking, get somebody else to drive you,
   e.g. R.A.C., A.A., taxis, or somebody from a garage.
   The 1967 law on drinking and driving is for the safety of
   everybody. Make sure you know it and keep within it.
2. If you have to take medicine or have injections, ask the doctor
   if and when it's safe to drive.
3. Don't drive if you are very tired.
   If you are going on a long journey, either share the driving
   or stop for rest and refreshment every so often.
4. Wear glasses if you need them.
   Get your eyes tested if you can't see as well as you used to.
   Make sure you can see as well at night as you can in daytime, comparatively speaking.
5. Either learn to control your temper whilst driving or don't
   drive.
6. Try not to drive if you are upset or depressed. If you must
   drive, try to control your feelings whilst driving.
   Never drive if you feel too miserable to care what happens.
   You **would** care if you killed a small child.
7. Take a refresher course if you want to start driving again after
   not driving for a long time.

Good drivers

1. Take enough lessons from a qualified instructor
2. Get plenty of practice

3. Have good driving ability.
4. Go on learning after they have passed their test.

They always:

Behave in a considerate and polite manner
Think ahead
Concentrate on their driving
Use their common sense
Dress for the job
Wear a safety belt even to just go "round the corner"

They never:

Drive on the wrong part of the road
Drive in the wrong gear
Drive at the wrong speed
Drive when they are not up to it.

Dressing for the job

What you wear can affect your driving.

Shoes —Proper driving shoes are safest. Loose, flimsy, high-
heeled shoes, wet shoes or no shoes at all are not safe.
Clothes—Must be comfortable—not too loose—not too tight.
Glasses—Very wide frames can stop you seeing properly. Special
anti-dazzle glasses help some people very much at night.
Gloves —It's safer to wear gloves, but they must not restrict
movement at all.

When to take extra care

Accidents may be avoided if drivers either don't go out, or drive
extra carefully, e.g. slower than they usually do, at the following
times:

Bank holidays
Christmas
When public houses close
Dusk and early morning
Very late at night
When special things are on in the district, e.g.
football matches, fetes, etc.
In wet, foggy or icy weather

and in the following places

On newly surfaced roads
Near schools and hospitals

In shopping streets
In villages
In areas which are new to them.

CHILDREN IN CARS

Small children are usually thought to be safest in the back of the car and:

(*a*) In a safety seat
(*b*) In a safety belt when big enough
(*c*) With the car doors locked

They should never ride:

(*a*) In the front of cars if they can't behave
(*b*) On somebody's knee

Remember even if a car just stops quickly or swerves suddenly, a small child can hit his head and be killed.

It is also important that small children:

(*a*) Have something to occupy them whilst riding
(*b*) Are taught not to shout at or touch the driver.
(*c*) Are taught not to play with the door handles (even if your car has safety locks, somebody else's may not).

OLD PEOPLE IN CARS

Remember old people cannot save themselves as younger people can.

(*a*) If the car brakes quickly or swerves suddenly an old person is likely to get badly hurt.
(*b*) In any accident an elderly person is likely to get badly hurt or worse.

It is therefore important:

(*a*) To get old people to wear safety belts. This is not easy as they are often nervous about being "tied in".
(*b*) To get them to ride in the back of the car.
(*c*) To make them as comfortable and safe as possible.
(*d*) Not to make them nervous by fast driving, etc. If they get too nervous they may do something which will **cause** an accident.

Safety seat and safety harness for children

This child is in DANGER

ACCIDENTS WHICH SHOULD NEVER HAPPEN

Accidents caused by the following things should never happen:

1. Alterations to improve the car's performance which are not done by a qualified person.
2. Stickers over the back (or side) windows which stop the driver seeing properly.
3. Dangling dolls and animals.
4. Fancy cushions propped up over the back window.
5. Awkward parking—suddenly popping in and out whilst cars are passing.
6. Accidents caused by animals not controlled in cars.
7. Children or animals being shut in cars and left there for long periods with no ventilation or not enough, becoming unconscious, or the car starting if left in gear. (You can buy a gadget which lets in air without making it possible for a child to climb out.)
8. Bad passengers who:

    (*a*) Block the driver's view through the back window.
    (*b*) Egg drivers on to go too fast.
    (*c*) Take the driver's attention off his driving.

9. Bad driving such as:

    (*a*) Driving too near the vehicle in front.
    (*b*) Speeding dangerously.
    (*c*) Overtaking when unsafe.
    (*d*) Turning right at junctions dangerously.

SPECIAL DANGERS

All drivers should know what to do to prevent or lessen accidents in case such things as these happen:

1. Steering going
2. Brakes going
3. Throttle jammed
4. Tyres blowing out
5. Windscreen shattering
6. Front or back wheels locking

They should also know what to do before such things happen:

1. Skidding on icy roads
2. Hitting water too fast.
      etc.

SAFETY EXTRAS

It is well worth trying to get anything which will:

(*a*) Help to prevent accidents happening
(*b*) Make injuries less serious if an accident does happen.

Such things as these help to prevent accidents:

1. Safety tyres
2. Safety belts (required by the law) properly fitted and in good condition
3. Disc brakes
4. Air conditioning
5. Comfortable driving seats—special cushions, etc.
6. Anti-dazzle inside mirrors
7. Wing mirrors, properly set
8. Windscreen washers
9. Sun visors
10. Safety locks
11. Easy to read instruments.

Such things as these help people not to get hurt at all or not so badly:

1. Collapsible steering column
2. Dished steering wheel
3. Extra padding.
4. For motor cyclists—safety helmets.

These things are necessary in case of accident:

1. First Aid kit
2. Fire extinguisher
3. Lamp
4. Emergency rations.

Note

Do your best to make sure that they can all be got at easily in an emergency.

IN CASE OF ACCIDENT

Many people need not die even in serious accidents if people (including children) who use cars know what to do in the case of an accident **before** one happens, e.g.

1. Learning general First Aid

2. Learning special First Aid rules for road accidents
3. Knowing how to get help
4. Knowing how to use the fire extinguisher.

❊ At School ❊

As everything is done to keep children safe at school, all they really have to do to keep safe is to:

1. Keep the school rules
2. Use common sense

A few reminders are:

1. Shoes—High heels, sling backs, sloppy shoes, and broken shoe-laces can all cause falls.

   A bad accident can happen if the fall is on the stairs, in the cookery room, science laboratory, etc.
2. Jewellery—Can cause nasty accidents in school. Metal bracelets can get very hot when cooking and burn the arm.

   Rings with stones in can cut somebody's face in the gym or whilst playing.

3. Long hair—Can get caught in washing machines or other moving equipment in cookery or boys' craft rooms.
It can also get set on fire over bunsen burners or stoves.

4. Disobedience—May be dangerous at any time but bad accidents sometimes happen when children disobey rules

On stairs
In science laboratories
In gyms
In cookery and craft rooms.

Most senior school equipment is the really professional equipment as used in trades, business, and research laboratories.
This means that adult works safety rules must be kept by children using the equipment.

5. Fooling about and showing off—These are only all right in safe places, but as they are usually done to show how daring the person is, the things which are done are either dangerous things or done in dangerous places.

Parents can do a lot to prevent school accidents:

(*a*) By obedience training at home
(*b*) By being interested in what is done at school
(*c*) By checking on shoes, hair, jewellery, knives, etc., before the child sets out. (Not always easy!)

 # At Work

Most large work places have their own safety rules. They have them printed and put up as constant reminders, but many little places don't warn their employees of danger at all.
Workers owe it to themselves and their families to avoid accidents whenever possible.
They should:

1. Obey all the safety rules of working and conduct for the safety of themselves and others, e.g. NEVER remove a safety guard from a machine.

2. Wear the correct safety clothes or equipment for the job.

3. Do the job carefully and in the right way at all times, especially on a new job.

4. Work tidily.
5. Never fool about or "skylark" at any time.
6. Report any faulty equipment at once.
7. Report even minor accidents and get them treated at once.
8. If there are no safety rules stated, it is up to every worker to:

   (a) Find out if there are any for the job.
   (b) Look round for any danger points and work out their own safety code.

Tiredness and ill health can cause accidents anywhere. It is every worker's responsibility to see that they get enough sleep and are fit for their job.

This responsibility is doubly important where the lives of other people are in the hands of the worker, e.g.

Drivers of public vehicles
Doctors and nurses
Chemists and dispensers
Anybody using dangerous substances or equipment near people.

Young people starting work

1. It is up to parents to get some idea of the conditions under which the girl or boy will be working:

   (a) Is the job itself dangerous?
   (b) Is there danger around, e.g. moving machinery, lorries, tractors, etc.?
   (c) What provisions are made for the worker's safety, particularly the young ones just starting?
   (d) Are there any health dangers?

2. It is up to employers to see that the school leavers are:

   (a) Told how to do the job correctly and clearly.
   (b) Told the safety rules and dangers.
   (c) Kept as safe as possible while training.

3. It is up to young people to:

   (a) Read, learn and obey the safety rules.
   (b) Behave in a safe and sensible manner so as not to cause an accident to themselves or other workers.
   (c) Do the job exactly as they are told.
   (d) Keep quarrels and bad feelings for outside work hours.

Young people in their first job should remember that whereas disobedience or stupidity at school will get them a bad mark or the cane, at work they may lose a hand or an eye, get badly burned, caught in a machine or killed—or cause equal hurt to a friend.

Safe Holidays

Holidays should be happy times and people should come home feeling fit and well, but sometimes they have accidents whilst on holiday and never come home again at all. This happens to many many children and often to grown-ups too.

Why is this?

1. The fresh air makes people more daring.
2. People want to "forget all the rules" when on holiday and "do as they like".

    This is all right until they forget **safety** rules and then they have an accident.
3. Many people plan everything for the holiday except their holiday safety.

Here are **ten general rules for Holiday Safety.**

1. Remember and keep all the "everyday" safety rules for

    Indoors
    Outdoors
    Travelling.

2. Have cars and cycles checked and repaired if necessary, before starting out.

    Share the driving if the journey is very long.
3. If you are doing something you haven't done before, like camping or sailing, get to know all about it before you go.

    Best to go with somebody who has done it before.
4. Buy the safest equipment you can. If you are using old equipment, get it checked for safety before you go.
5. Get to know all you can about the area you are going to and make a list of any danger spots. If it is a foreign country, make sure you know its road rules and take extra care as well.
6. Holiday health—doing too much, not getting enough sleep, eating unwisely, can all result in accidents or illness.
7. Make a list of "obedience rules" for the children. Make it short and make sure they keep them.

8. Decide not to take any risks.
9. Make sure all the family know how to get help if an accident happens, or if they get lost.
10. Make sure you have

    (*a*) All the children well "labelled" with their

Names
Holiday address
Home address
Any telephone numbers.

    Identity bracelets are best.

    (*b*) Proper First Aid kits for the car and for when you go without the car.
    (*c*) Repair kits for cars, cycles, and any special equipment.

If you are leaving the hotel, boarding house, camp or your own home, etc. for a whole day, it is important to

    (*a*) Tell somebody where you are going, especially if you are going to do something like climbing, sailing, etc.
    (*b*) Let them know what time you expect to be back. If you find you are not going to get back at that time, ring them up if possible to tell them.
    Good idea to keep telephone coins in your First Aid kit— not to be used for anything else.

"COME BACK SAFELY" HINTS

WATER

Some of the ways people get drowned are by:

Getting carried out to sea
Falling down holes or shelves
Falling out of boats
Falling off bridges, walls, etc.

Some of the reasons people get drowned are:

Bathing—Can't swim or float
Staying in the water too long
Swimming too soon after meals
Swimming alone
Swimming whilst in poor health

Diving in unknown water
Using unsafe equipment.
Boats—Can't manage the craft
Lack of, or poor life-saving equipment
Unsafe craft
Lack of knowledge—Tides, weather, beaches
Disobedience—Danger signs or instructions
Parents' orders
Fooling about—In boats, in the water, etc.

What to do?

Swimming

Swim parallel with the shore

1. Make sure all the family know how to float. (Not just for a few minutes.)
2. Make sure all the family know how to swim. (A few strokes is not enough.) Safer if they can life-save too. Even very small children can learn to float and swim.
3. Remember it's harder to swim or float in the sea than it is in the swimming bath.
4. Find out if there are:

Holes or shelves on the beach

Any strong currents
Weeds
Any other dangers, e.g. if you want to dive, is the water deep enough?

Check safety for rivers and ponds too.

5. Make sure you know exactly what time the tide starts to go out.
6. Don't let anybody swim:

    (*a*) Until 2 hours after a meal
    (*b*) For too long
    (*c*) If they are not well
    (*d*) If they are very tired
    (*e*) Alone—this is never safe for children and often unsafe for grown-ups too. No diving alone either.
    (*f*) Too far out or straight out. (Swim in line with shore.)
    (*g*) When the tide is going out (children particularly).
    (*h*) Near boats.

Swimmers who know they get cramp should never go too far out or swim alone. Remember, anybody may get cramp.

The person who is in charge of a group of children bathing must:

    (*a*) Not swim themselves
    (*b*) Watch the children all the time
    (*c*) Count them often

7. Danger signs:

    (*a*) Tell the children what signs to look for before they go on holiday.
    (*b*) Keep a look out for them when on holiday.
        Some signs are there all the time.
        Some are only put out when the sea is rough.
    (*c*) Make obeying these signs one of their "holiday obedience rules".
    (*d*) If you don't know what "safety and danger" signs are used where you are going, find out the first day!

8. Floats:

These include:

Mattresses
Animals
Boats

Water wings
Arm bands
Rings and tyres
Big balls
Pieces of wood, cork, polystyrene
Home-made "rafts"
    etc.

They can all cause somebody to drown.

(*a*) Non-swimmers can be taken out of their depth.

(*b*) Good swimmers can be taken further out than they can swim back.

(*c*) The air can come out of blown up ones. Then a small child can get very frightened and drown even in shallow water.

Look out—danger here!

They are so nice to use it seems a pity to make rules and children find rules hard to keep, but rules **must** be made.

(*a*) They should not be used by non-swimmers unless an adult who can swim is very close.

(*b*) They must never be used when the tide is going out.

It is safer

(*a*) To let children use them only in enclosed pools.

(*b*) To tie them by strong rope to something really firm (not a deck chair).

Even if you tie them up a grown-up must still keep watch.

The child may fall off.
The air may come out.
The rope may come undone.

Boats

1. Make sure **everybody** has a life jacket. Buy ones which conform to British Standards. Children must wear a life jacket **all the time**. Adults taking small children in boats **must** be able to rescue them if they fall in the water, i.e. the adult must be able to swim and life-save!

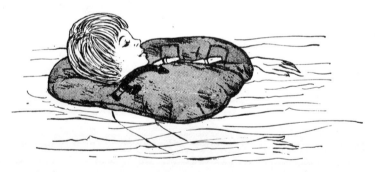

A well-designed life-jacket that keeps the head clear of the water

2. The boat and all the equipment must be safe, i.e. in good condition and work properly.
This includes

Fire extinguishers
Lights

Signals
Maps, charts etc.
Repair kit
First Aid kit

3. The person in charge of the boat and, ideally, other people too, must

   (*a*) Be fit and well—good eyesight also.
   (*b*) Know how to manage the boat properly.
   (*c*) Know how to swim and life-save.
   (*d*) Be able to give artificial respiration.
   (*e*) Know the local conditions, e.g. tides, weather, coast line, where coastguards are, etc.

4. All crew and passengers **must** obey the one in charge of the boat. Decide who is to be the "captain" before setting off.
5. Work out emergency drill and have practices too.
6. Before going out, let somebody know where you are going and what time you intend to get back. Don't forget to let them know **at once** if you land somewhere else.
7. Emergency food and water is always necessary if there is the smallest chance of people being in a boat longer than they expected.
8. Everyone should have warm and waterproof clothing.

The most dangerous way to go in a boat is, when somebody says, "It's a lovely day, let's hire a boat. I've been out once or twice before." Then to pile in without checking anything, life jackets, distress signals, etc., etc.

Anybody who is going for a holiday near water should decide before they go whether they are going in boats, even in little ones, and learn the safety rules before they start their holiday (e.g. "stay with capsized craft").

If children learn some of the real sailing rules and words they will apply them even in little boats and be safer as a result. They should never be allowed to play in boats unless an adult is present.

Many people forget that just as much care is needed on rivers and canals, for holidaymakers, as on the sea.

See last page for useful addresses.

Coastguards

There are coastguards on duty all day and all night all through the year.

By ringing 999 or asking the operator for "Coastguards" anybody can get help at any time for themselves or for others. Ring the Coastguards if:

1. You see a boat or a person in difficulty, e.g.

   On the water
   In the water
   Cut off by the tide.
2. If you are near the water and a child or a swimmer is missing.
3. If you are expecting somebody to arrive in a boat and they don't arrive.
4. If you are taking a boat round the coast, you can ring the coastguards, and all the coastguards on your route will check you round.

   Then if you fail to appear in any coastguard's area when expected they will look for you.
5. If you want to know about tides, weather, currents, or any local risks, you can ring the coastguards and they will tell you all you want to know.

   e.g. If you are taking a boat out
   If you are taking the family for a holiday in a place you don't know.

When you think how much is done to keep people safe, it is up to everybody to do all they can to:

(*a*) Get all the information they can about water safety.
(*b*) Keep all the safety rules.

Then they can enjoy their holiday on or by the water and be alive to go again next year.

CLIMBING

As with many other holiday accidents, a large number of climbing accidents need not happen. These rules can save lives:

1. Find out all you can about climbing before you go.
2. Find out all you can about the area you wish to climb in—before you go. Study maps carefully.
3. Until you are really good at it, arrange to go with a group plus a qualified guide.

4. (*a*) Get the right equipment
   (*b*) Get the right clothes and boots, etc.

The wrong ones many cause you to be killed.
The right ones can save your life, e.g. a safety helmet.
Bright coloured clothes make it easier to find you.

Take the trouble to find out from climbing clubs and experienced climbers which things are best for a learner.

5. It's safer to reckon that every climb might be difficult and prepare for it as if it will be, while you are learning.
   Always reckon on loose rocks and bad weather.
6. Believe what you are told about any difficulties which might arise even if you don't see how they can, e.g. how quickly the weather can get dangerously bad. (A waterproof coat or "rescue blanket" is always a must.)
7. Make sure **you** are well equipped in case you get lost. Don't rely on the compass, maps, whistle, torch, first aid things, and food somebody else is carrying, have your own too.
8. Make sure for yourself that somebody knows where your group is going and when they should be back.
9. It's usually safer not to split up the party.
   Finally,

   (a) Never judge mountains and hills by how beautiful they look from a distance on a lovely day.
   (b) Learn all you can on each climb—even make notes later.
   (c) Get your clothes and equipment in good order for the next one!

Write to the British Mountaineering Council for more information (see last page for address).

CAMPING

Find out as much as you can before you go.
Go for a short time to start with.
Practising in the garden is a good idea to start with.
Do all your preparations with an eye to safety, e.g.
Choose a safe area, especially if there are small children.
Make sure all the equipment is in a safe condition.
Don't take all the "old things" unless they are really safe, e.g. knives, tin openers, etc.
Make a set of camp safety rules.
Take the safest stove you can get.
Have one person in charge of the stove and its fuel.
Don't forget the First Aid box and emergency telephone money.
If you are travelling as well, take a compass and a map.

The site

Choose a safe spot as well as a nice spot.

Little children can get drowned in the smallest stream.

Don't camp under trees:

(*a*) They get struck by lightning
(*b*) They may fall on the tent in a high wind.

General safety rules

1. Keep all the "home" safety rules,

   e.g. Tidiness to prevent falls
   Hygiene to prevent illness
   Cleaning things, etc. in proper containers
   Proper rest times to prevent over-tiredness
   Don't drink stream water however good it looks.
   If you must, strain it and boil it first or use special tablets.

2. Protect small children from danger.

   Keep any water tanks firmly covered
   Guard any trenches
   Watch those ropes
   If there are several, "call a roll call" at meal times and bed-time.

Accidents which can easily happen whilst camping but which can usually just as easily be avoided are:

Fire
Falls
Children getting lost and falling into danger
Cuts
Drowning.

Fire

1. Be careful where you light the fire.

   Away from tents
   Away from dry grass, hedges, etc.
   Make sure the last fire is really out when you leave.
   Put water on it.

2. Be careful when you are lighting the fire.

   Don't sit or stand facing the wind.
   Don't lean over it to blow it.

Don't let small children help.

3. Using stoves:

Never use them in or too near tents.
Make sure they are sheltered from wind.
Never leave the rest of the fuel or box of matches near the stove.

Store fuel carefully

Away from tents
Away from food
Where children can't get at it.

Remember

Butane is explosive.
Paraffin is poisonous and bursts into flame easily.
Meta cubes are poisonous.
Take extra care not to put paraffin or methylated spirit into soft drink bottles. Thirsty people are not very careful.

4. Matches and cigarettes:

Never throw them down even if you think they are out.
Safer to put them in a tin with water in it.

5. Glass and tins:

Always bury them deep.

(*a*) Animals dig them up and can get badly cut
(*b*) Anybody can cut themselves on them
(*c*) Even small bits of glass can catch the sun's rays and cause a fire.
(*d*) Don't leave plastic bags or pieces anywhere. They make animals very ill.

6. If fire starts:

Send somebody for help.
Don't tackle big fires.
If you tackle a small fire, don't face any wind.
Make sure the rest of the fuel is out of the way.
Don't let small children help.

DAYS OUT

Many people don't think of safety when they take the family out for days or half days, but accidents can happen on short trips as well as on longer holidays.

It is important to keep all the safety rules already listed, as well as extra ones such as:

Keeping small children always in sight, especially in such places as fairs and zoos.

Note

In the country, always shut gates. If animals stray out of their fields, they can

(*a*) get hurt themselves
(*b*) cause road accidents.

 Leaving Home

Many young people leave home at quite an early age. They will be safer if

1. They have a reasonable place to live in

   e.g. Hostels
   With a family
   With relatives or friends of the family
   at least to start with.

2. They keep in touch with home
3. They join a church, or youth club or sports club
4. They know where to get help if things go wrong
5. They know how to look after themselves
   e.g. The general health rules for eating, sleeping, etc.
   How to look after their own room (saves getting turned out!)
   How to keep out of trouble—with the law—with boy friends or girl friends, etc.
   How to manage their money
   To take care of their belongings, papers, etc.
   How to get on a doctor's list
   etc.

Parents can do a lot to help
1. By keeping in touch with them

2. By tactfully keeping in touch with somebody who can keep an eye on the young person
3. By making sure they know the dangers of "going out into the world" without making them nervous or feeling as if they are being treated like babies
4. By letting them know they can come back if things don't work out.

Fire

 About Fire

Fire is NEVER funny
     NEVER a lark
     NEVER a good joke
Fire is **always** SERIOUS
     always DANGEROUS
Fire can KILL by BURNING
     KILL by SUFFOCATION
     KILL by SHOCK
     KILL by POISONING.

Which things burn? Here are just some things:

The bodies of **people**—Children, men, women
The **clothes** people wear—Cotton, silk, rayon, wool mixtures,
    winceyette, etc.
Many **toys** children play with—Wooden ones, some cuddly ones,
    some plastic ones.
Things houses are **built** with—Wood, plaster, fibre board, etc.
Fuels houses are **heated** with—Coal and coke, gas, oil, wood.
Things houses are **decorated** with—Paint, varnish, some plastics,
    polystyrene, etc.
Things houses are **furnished** with—Furniture, the wood and the
                         stuffing
                    Curtains, covers, cushions
                    Wooden beds, mattresses,
                    blankets, sheets, pillows.

How can things be made to burn?
By being lit with

Matches and other lighters
Electric sparks
The hot sun.

Some things will burn all by themselves without being lit by anything. See p. 242.

Some things will burn if they are left against hot pipes, e.g. clothes left airing on pipes too long.

How do fires start?

1. By **children** setting light to things.
2. By fires being left **unguarded** or not guarded well enough.
3. By **curtains** blowing on to stoves or candles.
4. By **smokers** throwing matches and cigarettes down when they are not quite out.
5. When electricity, gas and oil are not **used** properly.
6. When things which burn very easily are not **stored** properly.
7. When chimneys are not swept regularly.
8. When glass is caught by the sun's rays (e.g. mirrors left on window sills), etc.

How do fires spread?

1. When the things around burn easily.
2. If there is a wind or draught.
3. By the air around getting very hot. This hot air (and the smoke) rises and sets things alight as it goes.
4. By hot metals conducting heat to things which burn.

Remember

It isn't only flames which kill people.

People die very quickly when they breathe in SMOKE—It chokes and poisons.

People die very quickly when they breathe in HOT AIR.

 Preventing Fires

General rules

1. Use electricity, gas, solid fuel and oil carefully and correctly.

2. Make all the rooms, the loft, and passages safe from fire.
3. Check the garden, sheds and garages, make these safe too.
4. Cook carefully.
5. Don't cause fires by the way you run the house.
6. Buy things which won't burn, or won't burn easily.
7. Teach the children fire safety.
8. Make sure all the family know what to do if there is a fire.
9. Stand portable fires on something which won't burn.
10. Use non-flame materials to insulate pipes, lofts, etc., e.g. Fibre glass.

 # Using Fires

Most household fires begin with the fire which heats the home. Many of these fires need never happen if

1. All fires are properly guarded
2. They are in good working order.

The important subjects of planning and buying a safe heating system and keeping children safe from fire have been dealt with elsewhere in this book.

There are, however, still a few more points which will help to prevent fire accidents.

OPEN FIRES

Lighting

1. NEVER use paraffin, petrol, sugar or fat. Firelighters are safer.
2. NEVER use a sheet of newspaper to draw the fire up.
   A sheet of strong tin with a handle on does the job better and is safe **but**

   Don't leave it too long
   Do use an oven cloth to take it down!

3. DON'T leave the matches, firelighters, extra wood and paper near the fire whilst you are lighting the fire.
4. Take care when brushing the hearth, etc. not to set the brush and yourself on fire!
5. DON'T leave the fire for even one minute without the guard up, especially if there are children about.
6. Don't put ashes in cardboard boxes or on sheets of newspaper unless you are sure they are cold.

A covered carrier for hot ashes

Use a metal container or bucket (safer still if covered).
Take it out of the house straightaway.
7. Take extra care with gas pokers. Don't let them drop out. Remember they are still hot after being taken out.

At night
1. Don't make the fire up too near bed-time.
2. Don't leave a big blazing fire—bank it down with damp slack. (Pouring water on is a tricky job—steam and dust easily fly out into your face.)
3. Roll the rug away. Some people like to put a couple of tin trays down just in case.
4. Make sure the guard **and** a spark guard are up and securely fastened.
5. Shut the window and the door.

Windy weather
1. Don't pile the fire up too high. The wind can soon blow flames or sparks into a chimney fire.
2. Don't use wood on top of the fire.
3. Don't throw paper onto the fire. This is not safe at any time.

Chimneys
1. They should be swept
   At the beginning and end of winter—or at least before fire lighting time comes.
   When you move into a new house—even if the previous tenants say they have been done.
2. Sweep the lower part of "chimney" well at least once a week. Most people like to give a quick brush before lighting the fire.
3. If the fire starts being difficult to light for no apparent reason, get the chimney sweep to have a look. All sorts of things get down chimneys and can cause fires.
4. If the chimney still smokes after it has been cleaned get a builder to look at it.

Carrying coals

Carrying burning coals from one room to another is very very dangerous. For safety's sake it should **never** be done.

Mantelpieces

NEVER put any of these things on mantelpieces:

Mirrors
Clocks
Toys
Papers.

Many many children and grown-ups have been burned to death reaching for these things.

1. Even if the fire is very well guarded there is sure to be one moment when the guard is not there and that is the moment when somebody will stand too near the fire to reach for something off the mantelpiece or to look in the mirror.
2. In homes where there are no children some adults won't use a guard. In these homes

   (a) There's no sense in adding to their own risk of getting burnt by putting things which are in everyday use on the mantelpiece.
   (b) They add to the risk of visitors, children especially, getting burnt.

Rugs

These are dangerous:

Torn mats near fires
Rugs which burn easily
Fluffy mats which catch the feet.
For safer mats see "Buying for Safety", p. 30.

Guards

See sections on "Children", "Buying Safety".

OIL FIRES

These are extra likely to cause the house to be burnt down,

(a) Because the oil is highly inflammable.
(b) Because the flame is so near the oil.
(c) Because wherever the oil spills the fire will travel.

(*d*) Because unless they are in perfect condition and used perfectly correctly they are liable to burst into flame on their own.

(*e*) They may be knocked over (some can be fixed to the floor or wall now).

Apart from always being well guarded, safety rules for use are:

1. Always fill them out of doors. Use a safety filler can.

Best to do this out of doors—and DON'T SMOKE!

2. Wipe up any oil spilt on them. Best to use absorbent paper and put it in the dustbin at once.

3. When you bring them into the house, put them down carefully. If any oil spills on stove, floor or yourself, wipe it up at once.

4. Don't put them in a draughty spot. (They may flare up.) If they are put in the fireplace the opening must not be more than 20 square inches. (Safer to get an expert to check.) But remember the room must be ventilated.

5. Never put them near curtains or beds, never in cupboards or lofts.

6. Don't put them where people keep passing by.
7. Make sure they stand firm and on a base which can't burn, e.g. a metal tray.
8. NEVER light them:

   (a) When smoking
   (b) With oily hands.

9. NEVER put extra oil in them when they are alight.
10. NEVER carry them when they are alight.
11. DON'T let children light them even if they are able to.
12. DON'T leave them alight, even at "low", when the house is empty or when everybody has gone to bed.
13. Keep them in good order

   (a) Keep them clean
   (b) Wicks trimmed
   (c) Have them checked at least once a year and if they give trouble.

14. Always use the correct fuel.
15. Re-read the instructions sometimes!

Note

Most of these rules apply to using oil lamps too.

It cannot be said too often:

NEVER LEAVE A CHILD ALONE WITH AN OIL STOVE.

This is **very** difficult sometimes but children have been burnt to death whilst Mother has just gone to answer the door.

SMALL FIRES

These may be electric, gas or oil.
The danger lies in the fact that they **are** small.

(a) People think they don't matter so don't guard them properly.
(b) They put them in unsafe places where they can easily be knocked over.
(c) They run them from light and lamp fittings.
(d) They use them in silly ways, e.g. put them on chairs to dry hair.

It is as important to take as much CARE with small fires as with large fires.

They can cause a person to be burned to death or a house to be burnt down as easily as large fires.

CENTRAL HEATING

1. If there are children about

    (*a*) Put a fastener on gas boiler doors somehow.
    (*b*) Don't leave the door open to warm the room.
    (*c*) Don't let children see you light paper at the pilot light. (Safer not to do it!)

2. It's safer not to air clothes on the boiler door.
3. It's safer to let the Gas Board clean a gas boiler before you turn the heat on for the winter. (They charge.)
4. Don't leave beds, chairs, etc., leaning against hot radiators.

SMOKING

Careless smoking causes many of the worst fires. This is because the fires start very slowly and are not discovered until too late. They could all be prevented.

Remember, every cigarette and every match can cause a fire.

Safety rules are:

1. DON'T smoke

    (*a*) In or near the garage
    (*b*) When filling or cleaning oil stoves
    (*c*) When filling motor mowers
    (*d*) When using any other inflammable substances. See p. 244.

2. Lighting up

    (*a*) Make sure matches are out—some people break each one, by which time the match is out.
    (*b*) Don't throw them down.
    (*c*) Never use bits of paper, etc. lit at fires.

3. Ashes and ends

    (*a*) Make sure cigarette ends are really out before you leave them.
    (*b*) Use ashtrays when possible. If the ground is the only place, grind the end until it is really out.
    (*c*) Never stub cigarette ends out on things which can burn.
    (*d*) Don't leave lighted cigarettes around even on edges of ashtrays.

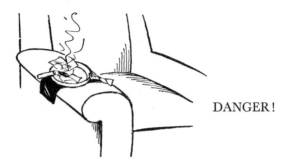

DANGER!

(e) Be careful where ash is dropped; even this can cause fires.

(f) Never put ashes, cigarette ends or matches in waste paper baskets.

4. Ashtrays

(a) Where there are smokers, including visitors, there must be plenty of ashtrays. Deep, covered metal ones are best.

(b) Put them near the smoker.

(c) Empty them before they overflow, perhaps to cause a fire.

(d) Don't let them be used for toffee papers, etc.

5. Pipes

(a) Must never be left anywhere unless they are really out.

Putting lighted pipes in pockets seems funny until an old gentleman gets burnt to death.

Keep an eye on old gentlemen's pipes.

(b) Must not be knocked out near anything which can be set on fire.

6. Extra care is needed:

(a) When people are tired.

NEVER smoke in bed.

Safer not to smoke in armchairs or settees if very tired and in the house alone.

(b) In cars

Don't drop ash or ends on the car floor—make sure passengers know where the ashtray is.

Don't throw cigarette ends out of the window, they can and do fall on things and cause a fire.

(c) In sheds

They are usually made of wood, often full of easily burned materials and don't always have windows.

It's safer not to smoke in sheds.

Keep an eye open for boys who practise smoking in sheds. Some have burned to death doing this.

(*d*) Outdoors

The danger of fire is particularly great in hot, dry or windy weather.

NEVER drop cigarette ends or matches just anywhere. Many people don't realize that short dry grass can burn and turn into a serious fire. The grass smoulders very slowly and the smouldering spreads and later bursts into flames.

RUBBISH

Much of the rubbish which collects in homes burns very easily, e.g.

Paper
Bits of wood and sawdust
Dust and fluff
Old batteries
Old paint and varnish tins
Oily and greasy rags and paper
Containers of inflammable substances
Old mattresses
Old furniture.

It seems silly to let old rubbish cause or help to burn a home down and possibly burn people to death too.

Main danger spots are:

Cupboards under stairs
Lofts
Cellars
Children's rooms
Lean-tos and sheds near houses.

Some people at least have a good clear out when spring cleaning, but, as many people don't spring clean these days, dangerous rubbish is likely to pile up.

The safest thing to do is:

(*a*) Throw all rubbish away at once.
(*b*) Before you put anything in the loft "in case it will come in handy" think, could it help a fire to burn?
(*c*) If you need to keep paper and wood for firelighting only keep a little indoors, the rest is safer away from the house.

(*d*) Cleaning and polishing rags.

Some polishes burn when in contact with air when no light is near them.

It is safer to

(i) Wash all polishing and cleaning cloths after use.
(ii) When you can't wash them, keep them in a tin with a lid on.
(iii) Never keep a collection of oily rags in the house anywhere. If directed to throw away the cloth after use, do so.

Even getting rid of rubbish may not be safe if not done properly!

Indoor fires

Don't throw these things on an open fire:

Dust—it explodes.
Greasy or oily things—they flare up.
Empty aerosols—they blow up.
Empty tubes with the lid on—they blow up.
Old rags—they smoulder—fumes can kill.

Remember—anything which explodes on the fire will fling burning coals and dust over the room and set the room on fire.

Dustbins

Don't set the dustbin on fire.

This is easily done if hot ashes are put in. Let them cool first.

This is most important where dustbins have to be kept very near to the house or even in the building.

Don't forget to carry ashes in a closed container.

In the garden

(*a*) Don't light incinerators or bonfires near the house, fences, sheds or garages.
(*b*) Don't throw dangerous things on. See "Indoor fires".
(*c*) Make sure bonfires are out at night. Pour water on them.
(*d*) If you have to go out and leave a bonfire burning, damp it down first.

AIRING CLOTHES

This has to be done in most homes and sometimes it has to be done quickly.

Fires caused by airing clothes usually happen

(*a*) By putting the clothes too near the heat.

(*b*) By leaving them near the heat too long.

(*c*) By using dangerous airing equipment.

Putting things too near the heat. Examples are:

(*a*) Airing things on the tops of cookers.

(*b*) Airing things in front or over all kinds of fires and boilers.

It is better not to air clothes like this.

If you have to do it, DON'T LEAVE THEM, even for one minute.

Leaving things too long

This may be done when:

(*a*) Clothes are left to air in another room

(*b*) People go out

(*c*) People go to bed

(*d*) Clothes are left to air on pipes or radiators or cisterns.

The best thing to do is:

(*a*) Put clothes-horses, etc., further away from the heat, if you are not going to be in the room all the time.

(*b*) When radiators are very hot, hang clothes near, but not on them.

(*c*) Don't forget them!

Equipment

The following are all dangerous:

(*a*) Lines fixed across mantelpieces

DANGER!

(*b*) Lines over cookers or portable fires
(*c*) Unsteady clothes-horses
(*d*) Homemade airing cupboards using ordinary portable fires and having no ventilation holes in the door and no extra guards. Airing cupboards are safer fixed by qualified electricians.

INFLAMMABLE SUBSTANCES

These include all kinds of things used for

Building   Cooking
Heating   Cleaning clothes
Decorating   Hobbies
Cleaning the house   Beauty care
                                 etc.

e.g.

Paints, Turps, Turps substitute, varnishes, paint strippers, solvents, linseed oil, etc.
Furniture polish, shoe polish, etc.
Paraffin, petrol, methylated spirit, clothes cleaning fluids, fire-lighters, lighter fuel.
Modern adhesives, photography liquids.
Nail varnish, hair sprays, perfumes.
Rags soaked in any of these things.
   etc.

Careful use includes:
1. Never smoking whilst using petrol, paraffin, nail varnish, etc.
2. Never using stain removers by a fire—remember pilot lights on stoves, boilers, water heaters, etc.
3. Never using aerosols—hair sprays etc.—where there is a fire—remember the pilot lights again.
4. Never filling lighters in front of the fire.
5. Not varnishing nails too near the fire.

Remember—vapours travel and burst into flame when they meet even the smallest light.

Careful storing includes:
1. Not keeping any inflammable things near the cooker or boiler or in any warm place.
2. Not leaving lighter fuel on the mantelpiece.
3. Storing cooking fats and oils in a cool place.

4. NEVER keeping petrol in the house.
   NEVER keep more than a gallon of paraffin in the house (none is safer).
5. NEVER storing petrol or paraffin just outside back doors upstairs or downstairs.
6. Not leaving aerosols on window sills where the sun can heat them up until they explode. Keep them in a cool place.
7. Not keeping polishes and other cleaning things in a warm place.
8. Always keeping paraffin and petrol in metal containers and always keeping the lid on firmly. (Under cover and away from the house.)

Take extra care:

1. To check hobby kits used by children or adults, e.g.

   (*a*) Chemistry sets—Is there anything which could cause a fire? Make sure it's kept away from the fire.
   Is the bunsen burner safe? Does it stand firm and have proper rubber tubing?
   (*b*) Photography—some liquids used are highly inflammable.
   (*c*) Construction kits—some adhesives are highly inflammable. Some of the materials are too.

2. To read all labels to see if the contents are inflammable.

SPECIAL TIMES need special care, e.g.

Celebrations
Wintertime
Leaving the house
Bed time.

Parties

Parties, especially children's parties, should be all fun and happiness, but not all parties are like this, sometimes a child gets burned to death.
   To prevent fire:

1. Make sure all fires are guarded, even at adult parties. Some people do drink too much and fall about.
2. Children's parties—be extra careful to have all fires guarded. Don't forget bedrooms, too.
   Although your child may be wearing a dress of "Non-flare" material, other children may not be.
   Make sure candles are firmly fixed.

3. The more paper things are used, the more care must be taken. Do a quiet tidy up of paper things as the party goes on.
4. Provide plenty of safe ashtrays and use big tins for paper baskets.
5. Keep an eye open for careless smokers during the party. Check the room and furniture before going to bed. Empty all the ashtrays too.

A dangerous game if there's no fireguard

Christmas time

Fire is likely to be caused by:

Decorations

Don't put them

1. Near light bulbs
2. Round the mantelpiece
3. Near any fire—remember wall heaters if you have them
4. In the kitchen. If the family use the kitchen as a living room, make sure decorations are not near the cooker or water heater, etc.

Trees

1. Never put candles on them.
2. Don't put them near the fire or draughts.
3. Check lights before you put them on the tree. Don't let decorations touch them.
   Turn them off when you go to bed.
4. Make sure the tree is safely planted in earth or sand in a well-balanced container.

Some people water the soil or sand every day. Remember, the tree and practically everything that goes on it will burn like fury if it catches alight. You cannot be too careful.

Wrappings

Get them into the dustbin as soon as you can. Not easy because children love them!

You can use foil and nylon ribbon for safer family parcels, but of course you can't control presents.

Mantelpieces

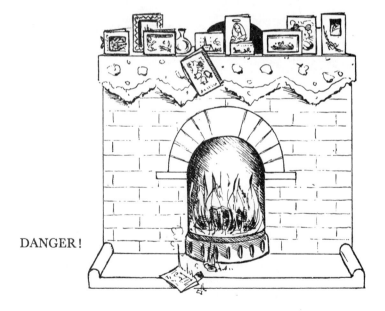

DANGER!

1. Don't put cards on them or hang them down the sides. Too dangerous.

2. Don't let children hang stockings for Father Christmas on them.
3. Don't put any pretty things on them that children may grab.
4. DON'T put rolls of cotton wool on even if it does look "Christmassy".

Don't make coal fires too big and don't forget a guard for any fire not often used.

Guy Fawkes Night

Fire danger starts as soon as children can buy fireworks or sparklers or coloured matches in the shops.

What can parents do?

1. Not let any small child touch any of them.
2. Not let any small child near the bonfire. Let them watch through a closed window.
3. Make rules for the older children:

    (*a*) No fireworks let off indoors
    (*b*) No fireworks to be let off until the night of November 5th. Great test of obedience here!
    (*c*) No fooling with fireworks at any time.
    (*d*) Read rules and directions before lighting any firework.
    (*e*) No attempts at making them.
    (*f*) Don't put them in pockets.

Make sure it's really out (it shouldn't have been so near the fence, either)

4. Bonfires

    (*a*) Well away from the house, sheds, fences, and garages.
    (*b*) Adult in charge.
    (*c*) No helping it with petrol, paraffin, etc.
    (*d*) Soak it with water before going to bed.
    (*e*) Keep the box of fireworks well away. (Lid on.)

Leaving the house

1. Going shopping

    (*a*) Don't leave oil stoves on.
    (*b*) Safer not to leave non-automatic cookers on.

2. Out for the day

    (*a*) Don't leave a fire.
    (*b*) Safer not to leave pilot lights on.
    (*c*) Unplug unnecessary electrical appliances.

3. Going away

    (*a*) Switch off electricity and gas at the mains.
    (*b*) Turn off pilot lights and taps on all gas appliances.
    (*c*) Put out open fires and boilers.
    (*d*) Close all inside doors.
    (*e*) Don't smoke when you make your last check-up round.

4. Moving out

    (*a*) Electricity and gas should have been turned off by the Board's men.
    (*b*) Make sure the last fire is really out—clear grate.
    (*c*) Don't smoke on last look round.
    (*d*) Close all windows and inside doors.

5. Moving in

    (*a*) Take care with any improvised cooking or lighting.
    (*b*) Get rid of packing paper quickly.
    (*c*) Take care furniture, etc. is not near any fire which may be lit.
    (*d*) Check very carefully before going to bed, until the house is straight.

Winter

1. Before the cold weather sets in:

    (*a*) Have chimneys swept.

(*b*) Check all heating equipment—have it repaired if necessary. Don't forget fire backs and boilers.

(*c*) Have electric blankets checked.

(*d*) Lag pipes—to prevent freezing—to prevent fire accidents
when thawing.

(*e*) Clear out rubbish.

2. Icy weather:

(*a*) If pipes freeze, DON'T use blow-lamps or portable fires to
thaw them.

(*b*) Never put portable fires in lofts.

(*c*) Don't leave oil stoves in bathrooms or lavatories. (Portable
electric fires must NEVER be put in bathrooms anyway.)

(*d*) Don't leave portable fires in unusual places unless you
have warned everybody first. Best to put a guard round
them too.

Safely to bed

1. Make sure open fires are out or banked right down.

2. Pull rug back. Some people like to put a couple of tin trays
down too.

3. Put guard up—unfixed guards can be knocked down by falling
coals. Add a spark guard for more safety.

4. Unplug all electrical appliances not in use, e.g. fires, radio,
television, etc.

5. Unplug electric blankets—check with directions.

6. Safer not to leave any oil heaters on.

7. Empty ashtrays—check no cigarette ends have been left on
chairs, etc.

8. Make sure no parts of the cooker are left on.

9. Close all doors. (Use an inter-com so as to listen for children.)

10. Close all windows apart from bedrooms.

 Taking Precautions

Even when you have done all you can to prevent a fire starting,
it still may happen.

Fire may be prevented from getting out of hand and people's
lives saved if everything possible is done to:

1. Prevent it spreading

2. Put it out

3. Get people out quickly.

To prevent it spreading

1. Don't feed it:
   (a) By leaving things which burn easily where a fire might start, e.g. near open fires, portable heaters, boilers, etc.
   (b) By buying things which burn easily when you could buy things which don't burn easily. See p. 30.
2. Don't fan it:
   (a) By leaving downstairs doors and windows open at night— or any unnecessary upstairs windows.
   (b) By leaving windows and inside doors open when you go out.
   (c) By rushing out and leaving doors open if a fire starts in the room you are in, and if you go out to phone.

To put it out

1. Work out the quickest way you can to ring the fire brigade. e.g. Arrange with a neighbour to use their phone.
   Check up on the nearest phone box.
2. Get some fire-fighting equipment for the home.

To get people out quickly

1. Work out the quickest way to get out from all parts of the house.
2. Practise getting out quickly before a fire happens.
3. Get some fire escape equipment.

EQUIPMENT TO GET

1. To give the alarm

A fire detector will let you know if fire starts anywhere in the house.

But

(a) They are too dear for many people.
(b) If you live in somebody else's house they may not let you fix it up.
(c) They do not detect smoke.

A more possible kind of fire alarm for most people is a DOG, especially if you train it to do the job.

2. To fight fire

Extinguishers—These can be bought to put out fires where:

(a) Only wood, paper, and cloth are burning

(*b*) Where flammable liquids, petrol, oils, greases and fats are burning.

Read the directions carefully and store in a cool dry place.

But

Domestic ones are usually only big enough for small fires.

Fire blankets—The best ones are really fireproof, electric shock proof, and acid resistant.

If proper extinguishers and fire blankets cannot be afforded, keep these things handy instead, upstairs and downstairs if possible:

(*a*) Buckets of water (Red plastic or painted red)
(*b*) Buckets of sand (Red plastic or painted red)
(*c*) A piece of army blanket about 1½ yards square. Fold it, roll it and tie it loosely.

If there is a garden hose, keep it where it can be got at easily.

3. For escaping

The main kinds of equipment which can be bought are:

1. Fire escape stairs
2. Ladders—fixed or portable
3. Cradles—for children, old or sick people
4. Webbing and fluffy rope types.

If you can't buy equipment, get ready

1. Something you could let down a baby or small child in from upstairs
2. An ordinary ladder (lightweight if possible).

The Fire Protection Association (address at end of book) and Fire Brigades will give anybody advice about buying fire fighting and fire escape equipment for the kind of house you live in. The important points about the equipment are:

1. The equipment must be handy, e.g. in kitchen and upstairs.
2. Small children must not be able to get at equipment.
3. Keep in good condition (makers will do this).
4. It must never be played with.
5. Make sure you get a big enough extinguisher. Make sure it's refilled as soon as possible after use.

WHAT TO DO

If people would stop to think how helpless they would be if fire broke out they would

(*a*) Do more to prevent fires
(*b*) Make sure they have the right things handy to put fires out.
(*c*) Make sure all the family knows what to do.

What to do may depend on

(*a*) When the fire is discovered
(*b*) Whether there is anybody to send for help.
(*c*) Whether there are small children in the house.

In any case the most important thing to remember is

SAVE LIFE BEFORE THINGS

This must still be done

(*a*) If you are poor and haven't many things
(*b*) If you are rich and have a lot of beautiful things.

If you are really poor and lose all your things through fire—people will help.
If you are rich and lose all your things—you can buy more—if you save your life.

The Fire Brigade

When a house is really on fire, everybody knows it's time to send for the Fire Brigade.
At other times people are not always sure if they should call the Fire Brigade or wait.
The Fire Brigade should be called the MOMENT fire STARTS TO BURN somebody's clothes, some thing, or you can see it's likely to.

(*a*) The Fire Brigade don't mind if the fire is out before they get to it.
(*b*) They will check that the fire is really out. (Fires often start up again later.)
(*c*) You don't have to pay.
(*d*) They don't make unnecessary mess.

In all cases of real fire starting, the rule is:

CALL THE FIRE BRIGADE

Note

It's often safer to go out and phone even if you have your own telephone. (Shut the door behind you.)

9—SFYF

Some "What to do" examples

1. If somebody's clothes catch fire, which should you do first, try to put them out or call the Fire Brigade?

PUT THE FLAMES OUT FIRST
CALL FIRE BRIGADE AND AMBULANCE

If there is somebody to help, they can get help as soon as you can manage.
To put the flames out:

(a) Lay the person down
(b) Roll him in a rug, blanket, big coat, etc.

Note

If you catch fire yourself and you are alone

(a) DON'T RUSH OUT
(b) Wrap yourself in something and/or roll on the floor.

2. If you are alone in the house with no phone and something is **really** burning, what should you do?

GET OUT QUICKLY (don't wait to dress)
SHUT THE DOOR BEHIND YOU
CALL THE FIRE BRIGADE (from outside)
DON'T GO BACK IN

3. If a fire has only just started burning things and you are alone in the house with little children and no phone, what should you do?

GET THE CHILDREN OUT QUICKLY (as they are)
DON'T GO BACK IN
CALL THE FIRE BRIGADE

4. If you are trapped by fire in a building, what should you do?

GET INTO THE NEAREST ROOM
SHUT THE DOOR
PUT THINGS AT THE BOTTOM OF THE DOOR
GET TO THE WINDOW
SHOUT FOR HELP

Notes

(a) Putting things at the bottom of the door is to keep out smoke and flames.

(*b*) Use rugs, carpet, mattress, pillows, cushions, etc.
(*c*) If you can soak them with water, better still.

5. What should you do if there is smoke all around but no flames, e.g. if somebody has been smoking in a bed or chair?

   (*a*) Get everybody else out
   (*b*) Soak a tea towel with water (or other material big enough to tie round your head)
   (*c*) Tie it round your nose and mouth
   (*d*) Open the door very carefully
   (*e*) Crawl across the floor to the person. (Less smoke on floor.)
   Very smoky? Crawl round the walls.
   (*f*) Drag the person out into the open.
   (*g*) Apply artificial respiration. Send for ambulance or doctor.

   If you manage to bring the person round yourself they must still be seen by a doctor.

   What about the Fire Brigade?
   The rule is still "Life before things".

   If there is somebody about they can call the Fire Brigade to start with. If you are alone you save life first and then call the Fire Brigade. Unless the person is in a very difficult part of the building to get to.

6. If a door is shut and you think or know there is something burning on the other side, should you open the door quickly and look? NO.

   What should you do? FEEL THE DOOR.

   (*a*) If it is warm it means there is a lot of heat and smoke ready to rush in.
   (*b*) If it is not warm—lean against it and only open it a very very little.

   Either call the Fire Brigade or follow the "Trapped by Fire" rules.

7. If a fire has **got a hold** on anything, should you try to put it out yourself?
   Not until

   (*a*) EVERYBODY ELSE IS OUT OF THE HOUSE
   (*b*) THE FIRE BRIGADE HAS BEEN CALLED
   (*c*) YOU ARE SURE YOU HAVE A WAY OF ESCAPE.

Then, only if

(*a*) You know what to do. (This depends on what is burning.)
(*b*) You have the equipment handy.
(*c*) The fire is not too big.

How to do it.

1. Wood, paper, cloth—use water.

   (*a*) Soak everything round the fire.
   (*b*) Soak the fire at the bottom.

2. Electrical things

   (*a*) If they are unplugged—water.
   (*b*) If not unplugged—special fire extinguisher.

of course unplug or switch off at mains if you can.

3. Oil, petrol, paints, varnishes

   (*a*) Special fire extinguishers best.
   (*b*) Hose (spray on) next best.

4. Portable oil heaters

   (*a*) Water—stand at least 6 feet away
   (*b*) Special fire extinguisher.

5. Chimney on fire

   (*a*) Call the Fire Brigade at once (no charge)
   (*b*) Make sure everybody is ready to get out quickly if necessary
   (*c*) While you are waiting, if there is no danger:

   > Roll the carpet back
   > Move the furniture back
   > Close the fire's ventilator
   > Close the door and windows
   > Check the walls of any other rooms which share the chimney. If they are hot, move any furniture away.

6. Fat pan on fire
   Turn off heat.
   Smother it with damp (not wet) cloth or with sand, earth or fire blanket.
   Don't carry pan outside or put it in the sink.

Note

If ever you do try to put a fire out before the Fire Brigade comes and you have to go out and get more water, etc., close the door when you go and open it carefully when you come back.

"THE FAMILY MUST KNOW"

One of the biggest dangers when fire breaks out is PANIC.
When people get panicky they can't think clearly and often do things which put their lives in danger, e.g. rushing back into a burning house to get something which may not even be important.
To prevent panic in case of fire there are some things a family must know beforehand.

1. The main dangers of fire.
2. The main fire rules.
3. That SMOKE MEANS FIRE.
4. The quickest way out.
5. What to do in particular situations.
6. How to call the Fire Brigade.
7. How to use equipment.
8. How to turn off gas and electricity.

What fire does

Flames burn
Smoke chokes
If you breathe very hot air you die
Fire spreads very quickly
Fire rushes up stairs
Smoke and heat rise.

The "Fire Five"—the main fire rules

"GET OUT QUICK"
"NEVER GO BACK"
"LIFE BEFORE THINGS"
"CALL THE FIRE BRIGADE"
"NEVER OPEN A WARM DOOR"

The quickest way out

ESCAPE ROUTE I—This must be worked out for each room, especially bedrooms and upstairs rooms.
ESCAPE ROUTE II—In case the first way is blocked.
A good idea (as used in some schools) is to print the escape route from each room on a card (in plastic cover).
The card is put in a place where nobody can miss it, e.g. by light switch.

Family Fire Drill

1. What to do if

> Your own or somebody else's clothes catch fire
> You are trapped by fire
> You wake up and smell smoke
> You see a fire start.

2. How to get out of the house quickly by day or night.
These must be learnt by everybody and practised.
Also need to:

(a) Decide on a Family Fire Signal
(b) Practise calling 999 (PRETEND).
(c) Choose a place to meet outside the house after getting out (counting everybody too).
(d) Practise using and replacing equipment correctly.

Where there are children there will also have to be rules like

(a) No false alarms
(b) No practising certain things without permission
(c) No playing with equipment

Don't forget

Fire extinguishers used for practice must be refilled at once.

Extra Notes

1. If you live in somebody else's house or blocks of flats, it may not be possible to put fire equipment where you would like to, or even do real escape drills.
   The best thing to do in this case is to

   (a) Get advice on fire safety from the local Fire Brigade—anybody can do this.
   (b) Try to make the place as safe as you can in case anybody gets trapped in it.
   (c) Take extra care not to start a fire.
   (d) Train the family in fire safety as much as you can.

2. Some people get burned to death trying to save valuables and special papers. Much worry and perhaps loss of life can be saved by putting these in the bank.
   If you don't put them in the bank, use a strong (not too big) metal box, but it will have to be put somewhere that you can get to easily in an emergency. **But** if you forget it don't rush back into a burning house for it.

Crime

 Protecting the House

There are usually three ways burglars can get into a house. They may:

(*a*) Be invited in
(*b*) Walk in
(*c*) Break in.

They break in through:

Doors
Windows
Skylights.

To prevent burglars getting in you have to:

(*a*) Be careful who you let in
(*b*) Make sure all your doors, windows, and skylights have good locks, etc.
(*c*) Remember to fasten all windows, skylights and doors when you go out.

WHAT TO DO

Callers—Don't invite people in if you are not sure who they are.

1. The best rule is NEVER open the door to a complete stranger in the daytime, in the evening, or at night.

2. If you do open the door because you were expecting somebody else,

   (*a*) Never open the door wide

   (*b*) Keep the safety chain on if you have one

   (*c*) Find out who they are. If you are not satisfied, ask them to call another time, even if they show you identity cards. Find out if they are genuine before they come again.

3. If you are alone in the house, it's safer **never** to open the door at once.

   Call through it—

   If it's someone you know, all right.
   If it isn't, ask them to call back.

   Then, look through the window to see—

   What they look like
   Any car number.

4. If the caller does seem odd it's best to let the police know at once. Give them the description and any car number too.

5. Even in the case of everyday tradesmen, it's better to shut the door when you go to get the money to pay them, etc.

6. The rule for children alone in the house is, "Don't open the door to anybody at all."

Remember, burglars don't look like burglars.

They look like:

   Nice couples, or single people, looking for rooms
   Nice lads looking for odd jobs
   Nice women with children
   Meter readers, window cleaners, workmen
   Policemen, vicars and agents
     etc.

They say they have come to:

   Check televisions, central heating, etc.
   Make market research surveys
     and so on

They may just come to look round and burgle your house a few days later!

Open doors—are an easy walk in for thieves.

1. Never leave the front or back doors open while you "go round to the shop" or "pop in next door".

2. It's not a good idea to leave the doors open whilst you do the garden, etc. if you can't see the door and you are alone.

3. Hot days are awful to work in but if the doors are left open and you are "hoovering" upstairs alone in the house you wouldn't hear anybody coming in.

Open windows—make an easy climb in.

Burglars can get through smaller windows than people think. People forget there are little burglars as well as big ones.
They can get through:

Small lavatory windows
Small pantry windows
The little fanlight windows at the top of big windows
Skylights.

It's always safest to:

1. Shut all the windows and any skylights before you leave the house empty even for a short time. The burglar can be in and out in 5 minutes.

    Do this even if you live upstairs. Don't forget a "window cleaner burglar" may come complete with ladder!

2. At night:

    (a) Make sure all windows are shut, including bathroom, lavatory, etc.
    (b) If you want fresh air in the bedroom either:
        Fit a window lock which will secure the window open
        or Get a special ventilator fitted
        or Have a grille, or bars fixed

Closed doors and windows

Burglars will break in through these very easily if

(a) Windows are not fastened securely
(b) Doors are not locked.

They will still get through them easily if

(a) The windows have only ordinary fastenings
(b) Doors have ordinary locks.

Many of them will be put off if

(a) You fit safety locks on to windows
(b) You screw down windows you need not use.

(*c*) You fit safety locks on doors.

Better still to have two locks 2 feet apart. Remember this includes back doors and french doors, as well as front doors.

If they do get in you can still check their progress by

(*a*) Fitting safety locks and bolts to inside doors
(*b*) Training a dog to give you a warning.
(*c*) Make sure all doors and windows are secure when the family are in bed or the house is empty. (There are people who fit special locks and don't use them!)

Special times

Are you sure the back door is locked?

Take extra care to fasten doors and windows securely in the daytime or after dark when:

Watching television
Listening to radios or record players
Enjoying parties
Celebrating Christmas, birthdays, or Guy Fawkes' night
Having a nap
It's foggy, windy, or snowy.

At all these times, burglars can enter houses without people knowing, take what they fancy and escape.

Neighbours

It is up to everybody to report to the police any odd happenings or suspicious characters which may mean somebody's house is about to be, or is being, burgled.

These kinds of things are always happening:

Removal vans taking out people's furniture
Men removing televisions, washing machines, etc.

One day it may be a neighbour's home being burgled, another day it may be your own.

When the house is empty

These advertise that the house is empty

Many people **tell** burglars which is the best time to call, e.g. they

(*a*) Put notes on doors saying "Back in half an hour".
(*b*) Let everybody know they are "never in on Tuesdays".
(*c*) Have bread, etc. left on doorsteps and window-sills.
(*d*) Put adverts. in local papers and shop windows saying "Call after 6.30 p.m." This often means that nobody will be home until that time.
(*e*) Let it be known when they have gone on holiday.

Remember

1. When you go out:

 (*a*) Never leave the key hidden—thieves always find them. It's safer to leave it with a neighbour you can trust.
 (*b*) Get a neighbour to take in bread, parcels, etc.
 (*c*) Leave some room lights on in the evening. If it's possible to see through the front door or letter box, don't leave the hall light on.

2. When you go on holiday:

 (*a*) Cancel milk, bread, and papers.
 (*b*) Put any valuables in the bank.
 (*c*) Let the police know.
 (*d*) Ask neighbours to keep an eye on the house.

Some people like to leave the telephone off the hook too.

Extra hints

1. Don't leave ladders handy for burglars to climb. (Put it in the garage or chain it up securely but remember you could need it in case of fire).
2. Try not to leave tools out which they can use to break windows.
3. Slimy anti-climb paint is handy for painting on easy to climb pipes.
4. If you get bogus telephone calls, report the matter to the G.P.O. They will intercept all the calls.
5. Keys—If you move, have new locks put on the doors. Somebody may still have keys to the old locks.
    If you lose a key it's always safer to change your lock. NEVER leave your key in the lock outside!
    Make sure children have a safe place to carry their key.
6. Teach children to check that windows and doors are shut properly if they are last out.

Don't leave things about to help burglars

BUYING PROTECTION

There are many things which you can buy to help keep burglars out. Here are some of them:

For doors

1. If you have glass panels in your outside door, fix a metal grille behind it. Some grilles are made that look quite ornamental.
   Burglars often cut a piece of glass out so that they can reach the lock from the inside.
2. Safety chains should be fixed on all outside doors and are not too dear to buy.
3. Door-optics can be fixed to doors so that you can see who is outside but they can't see you.
4. Lights over front, back and side doors mean the burglar has to risk being seen.
5. Safety locks make it much harder to open a door. Fix them on front, side, and back doors.
6. Safety padlocks and bars to keep the contents of garages and outside premises safe.
7. Safety bolts for the key side and hinge side of doors.

For windows

There are special locks and bolts for all kinds of windows, e.g.

Wood framed casements
Metal framed casements
Sash windows
Skylights.

Glass

Specially toughened glass is obtainable for doors and windows. "Triplex" and "Pilkington" are just two makers.

Doors and windows fitted with safety bolts and safety glass would deter pretty nearly all ordinary burglars.

Alarm systems

There are firms which will work out a complete system for your home by, for example:

Wiring doors and windows
Putting pressure mats by doors and windows and on stairs.
Fixing connecting wires to the local police station.
Fitting telephones with automatic 999 dialling.

If you can't buy complete alarm systems or rig the house up with safety locks, bolts, glass, etc., you have to:

(*a*) Be extra careful not to give burglars the chance to break in.
(*b*) Work out an alarm system of your own.
    Noisy gates and doors and creaking floorboards may be better left!
    Anything which will bang or clang loudly can be fitted to doors and windows and put in odd places.
(*c*) Dogs (and even birds and cats) are useful as alarm givers.

 Protecting Valuables

"Valuables" here includes anything which is worth a lot to the owner and which can be easily carried away by a thief, e.g.

Money
Jewellery
Cameras
Small radios

Watches
Cheque books and Post Office books

They also include

Important papers
Things which may not cost a lot of money but mean a lot to the owner.

An invitation to thieves

It is safer:

1. Not to carry a lot of money or keep a lot of money in the house. Keep it in the bank.
2. Never to leave handbags, purses, or wallets out of your sight even for one minute.
3. If you don't wear your jewellery often, keep it in the bank.
   If you do wear it:
   (a) Don't leave rings or watches on wash basins even for one minute.
   (b) Don't flash it around unnecessarily.
4. Never to leave money for tradesmen on steps, etc.

5. Not to leave valuables in or with clothes when you—
   Change at work
   Take your jacket off when you wash
   Take your coat off in a restaurant
   Change in the hospital out-patients department
   Change at the swimming bath
   Have your hair done.
6. To use lockers for clothes at work if there are any.
   To hang your coat, etc. where you can see it in cafés, etc.
7. Never to leave valuable things near windows at home. To do so gives thieves ideas. If you leave the windows open too you are asking for trouble.
8. Never to leave money, jewellery, etc. around when workmen come in to do jobs.
9. To keep important papers in the bank.
10. To look after your handbag, even in church.

Make a note of

(a) Any number on your things
(b) The make, appearance, etc.

Then if you lose them you can give the police a good description.

Sending valuables

If you have to send valuable things, make sure they are

Registered
Insured
Properly parcelled
Sent the safest way.

Shopping

Extra things to remember are:

1. Don't leave your purse in an open basket or in an easily got at pocket.
2. Don't leave your handbag or purse in the pram if you have to leave the pram anywhere.
3. Don't let small children carry your handbag.
4. Never put your purse or handbag down on the counter or in the self-service basket or trolley.
5. Make sure your handbag is always closed. If the catch is weak, take extra care it doesn't come open without your knowing.
6. Take extra care of your things in crowds and queues.

Mummy's handbag isn't
really safe with a
young child

Too easy for anyone to grab that purse

7. Don't leave your handbag, etc. where you can't see it when
   you are trying on clothes.
8. Take care of your handbag and cheque book when signing
   cheques in busy shops.
9. Count how many parcels you have and make sure you have
   them all when leaving cloakrooms or getting out of trains and
   buses. Don't let anybody leave with your parcels!

Don't put your
handbag down in
a shop even for a
moment

Travelling

The most important things to remember when travelling with valuables are:

Don't let anybody know you have got them.
Don't let them out of your sight.
Don't carry valuables in flimsy containers.

1. Don't talk in a loud voice about how much money you have with you. (Best not to carry more than you have to.)
2. Don't put your main luggage or hand luggage or briefcase down where you can't see them even for one minute, e.g.

   (a) When buying tickets, sweets, cigarettes, etc.
   (b) In cloakrooms, waiting rooms, tea rooms.

3. Don't leave luggage containing valuables unattended on luggage racks or train corridors.
4. Make sure all luggage is easily recognizable, has strong locks and is kept locked.
5. If possible, put valuable things in the kind of hand luggage which you can have with you all the time.
6. Keep wallets, etc. in inside zipped pockets and take care in crowds, in trains, on platforms, etc.
7. Don't leave valuables in cars if you can help it. If you must, make sure you

   Close the windows, including the quarter lights.
   Lock the doors
   Lock the boot
   Don't leave the valuable things where they can be seen easily.

8. Never leave handbags or shopping, etc. on bicycle handlebars, and don't leave them, or anything else valuable, in the saddle-bag when you leave the bicycle.

Don't leave valuables obviously in your car

To guard against cars and cycles being stolen

1. Don't leave them in badly lit and lonely places if you can help it.
2. Have an anti-theft device fitted on cars. Some insurance policies insist on you doing so if the car is not garaged at home. The police will be glad to give you any advice you need.
3. Bicycles should be chained round the wheel and frame and locked. Take the key with you. If it does get stolen, you must be able to tell the police exactly what the bicycle looks like and what the frame number is.

Protecting Children

It is the duty of all parents to do all they can to see that their children are

Kept safe from criminals and unbalanced people.

Children have to be taught how to avoid being molested, in the same way as they have to be taught how to avoid being run over.

Teach them never to:

1. Talk to strangers (men or women)
2. Go with strangers (men or women)
3. Take money or sweets from them
4. Get into their cars
5. Go into houses, sheds or garages.

Danger from a stranger!

Even if they know the person, tell them never to do any of these things straight away, but always to say "I must ask Mummy first". Don't forget that people who intend mischief to children know how to get round them by offering to show them (or give them) things they like, e.g. kittens, flowers, cakes, trains, etc. You have got to explain this to children as well as just saying "Never go with strangers".

It is also up to parents to do all they can to make sure that younger children

1. Are not out alone after dusk.
2. Don't play in deserted places (even with one or two others).
3. Learn how to tell the time as soon as possible—tell them not to ask strangers the time.
4. Don't have to come home from school, etc. alone even in the daytime.

   Remember to warn them against people who say they have been sent by the child's parents to take the child home.

Extra precautions are

1. To tell the child to tell his parents, teachers, or a policeman if anybody does try to take him away.
2. To teach him to notice what the person was wearing—this can be practised at any time.
3. To tell him to remember (or write down) the stranger's car number.
4. For parents to keep a tactful eye on any situation where a small child begins to be often in the company of a youth or older man even if the person is known to the parents or is "a married man with children".
5. For parents to make a strict rule that children come home from school first before going out to play.

   This is difficult if both parents are working.

Exactly how parents teach these things depends a lot on the child. Although it is important that the child should not be made frightened of all adults or "terrified of men" it is more important that the child is kept safe.

When the child doesn't come home when expected, it's safer to tell the police AT ONCE.

If the child returns or is found half an hour later, let the police know straightaway.

Older children

By this time they should have learnt all that has just been said, but it will be necessary to:

1. Teach them enough about sex to keep them safe.
2. Warn them not to accept lifts from strangers even if there are two or three youngsters together.
3. Warn them not to wait for friends in lonely, ill-lit places.

Learning "Judo" can be an additional safety measure for girls!

Sending children shopping

Somehow this doesn't seem the same as "sending the child out alone", but of course it is. Children can be enticed away on the short journey "round to the shop" as easily as they can get run over.

The safest thing of course is never to send small children shopping, but in many families the day comes when there is nobody else to send. What to do?

1. Tell the child to go "straight there and back".
2. Don't forget the child is out.
3. Look out for them when they should be on their way back. (No need to let them see you.)

If possible, don't send children out with large sums of money, they are safer without it.

Sending children to school

As well as doing their best to see that their children keep the "Road Safety rules" and "Safety from Strangers" rules it is up to parents to keep their children safe from thieves.

General rules for this are:

1. Don't let children take more money than is necessary.
2. Don't let them wear valuable jewellery. Keep an eye open for "borrowing without asking"!
3. Don't let them take other valuable things to show off to their friends.
4. Make sure that all their belongings are labelled.
5. Train them to look after their things.

By keeping to these rules, parents will also be doing a great deal to prevent petty pilfering amongst the children themselves.

Children travelling

Many children have to travel long distances to school and it is wise to warn them of other dangers, besides "not hanging out of train windows" and to tell them what to do, e.g.

1. Not to draw attention to themselves by loud behaviour.
2. Not to draw attention to themselves by the way they sit.
3. To travel in carriages where there are several people, not where there is just one person or nobody—to change carriages if necessary.
4. Not to allow themselves to be drawn into conversation by strangers.

Protecting the Family Business

As far as the building is concerned the same precautions can be taken as for houses—security locks, bolts and padlocks for all fasteners of doors and windows, the use of toughened glass, grilles or bars for windows, skylights and door panels, and good alarm systems.

Extra precautions are:

1. Leaving the place lit up during dusk and darkness.
2. During business hours, keep the money and till in a place where thieves can't get at it easily.
3. Not leaving the premises empty and unlocked even for a few minutes, especially where money is kept.
4. If you work alone in the shop, try to arrange things so that you don't have to turn your back too often!
5. Not leaving customers or enquirers alone where money or other valuables are kept.
6. Not leaving small children in charge even for a short time.
7. Don't make it easy for children to steal.
8. Using well-placed mirrors to prevent petty pilfering.
9. Bricking up unnecessary windows and doors.

Money

1. Ideally this should be put into the bank or night safe at least before the business is closed for the evening.

   If the premises are closed for lunch and quite a bit of money has been taken it's safer to bank before lunch as well as in the evening.

   Very young or elderly people shouldn't carry large sums through the streets.

   Never call out "I'm just off to the bank", and don't go exactly the same way every day.
2. If the money is not banked it should be put in a safe and not just in a "safe place", and the key should not be left in the business part of the premises.

   The best safes are the ones that burglars can't find or can't carry away.

   Lighting safes up is thought to put off burglars but not if they can put the light out or if the safe is not connected to a burglar alarm.

3. Take extra care at Christmas time and just before the holiday season.
4. If you go away let the police know.
5. Don't let casual employees know too much, they might have only come for information.

If you are new to business it is wise to ask the police for advice about safeguarding the premises, the money and any other valuables.

 # The Police Will Help

Before trouble

Many crimes could be prevented if people would:

1. Ask the police for advice (and take it) on such matters as protecting homes, valuables, businesses, cars, etc.
2. Take as much care as possible of themselves, their children and their possessions.
3. Report suspicious-looking prowlers.
4. Report even mild unpleasant attentions paid by strange men to women. (To get away with these is likely to make them bolder to commit more serious crimes.)

5. Report queer telephone calls to the G.P.O. and the police too if necessary.
6. Teach children to "ask a policeman" if they get lost.

After trouble

The drill is:

1. Call 999 at once.
2. Keep as calm as possible.
3. Give information clearly, e.g.

    Address—for burglaries, etc.
    Where you are
    Description of person
    The colour and type of clothes
    Any car number
    The time
    Any previous happenings which now look suspicious.

Learning to be observant and teaching children to be so too can be very useful if ever you become a victim of some crime.

 Children and the Law

Much can be done to cut down crime by training children to know and keep the law. What can parents do?

They can teach them to:

1. Be honest in all they do or say.
2. Respect other people and their property.
3. Use their leisure time in useful and interesting ways instead of having whole days and evenings with "nothing to do".
4. Manage money (saving and spending wisely)
    Manage time (planning)
    Manage themselves (self-control)
    Manage other people (getting on with people)
5. Work hard and play hard.

They can make sure children know:

1. The law

    What the laws are
    When the law is broken
    Punishments
    "Side effects" of convictions.

2. The dangers of

Drinking
Taking drugs
Promiscuity

Before they meet up with them.

They can help them by:

1. Making them feel

Secure
Wanted
Needed
Free (not smothered but not uncared for either).

2. Taking an interest in

What they do
Where they go
Who they go with.

If parents don't know or care what children do with their spare time children can easily—

Be led into crime
Drift into crime.

3. Being neither too soft nor too strict with them.
4. Remember these people will help **before** real trouble occurs:

Youth leaders
School teachers
Ministers
Probation officers
The Police
Psychologists
    etc.

Parents should:

(*a*) Take an interest in the child's school career.
(*b*) Keep in touch with the organizers of any groups to which the child belongs.
(*c*) Do their best to see that the child gets the right job for the child when he or she leaves school.

Some laws children should know:

1. They must not be sold:

Fireworks if they are under 13

Cigarettes if they are under 16
Guns if they are under 17
Alcoholic drink if under 18 (in public houses or licensed
premises).

2. They must not—

Drive a motorcycle under 16
Drive a car under 17
Smoke in streets or other public places under 16 (cigarettes,
etc., can be taken away if they do).

3. Boys of 16 and over commit an offence if they have intercourse
with a girl under 16.

4. They cannot—

Marry under 16 (in England)
They must have parent's consent if they are under 18.

They commit an offence if they do the following:

Steal from other children or grown-ups.
Hit other children or grown-ups.
Make a nuisance of themselves outdoors, e.g.

Make too much noise
Hang about and refuse to move
Fight
Annoy people in any way
Go on people's land without permission.

Keep things they find
Damage public or private property on purpose.
Let off fireworks in public places.
Carry knives or other weapons or things to harm people.
Travel without a proper ticket.
Forge things.
Put things on railway lines.
Go off in other people's cars or motor bikes without their
consent.
Help other people to break laws.
Set fire to things on purpose.
Refuse to take a breathalyser test when old enough to drive.

Useful Addresses

BRITISH MOUNTAINEERING COUNCIL. c/o Alpine Club, 74 South
   Audley Street, London, W.1.
BRITISH CANOE UNION. 26–29 Park Crescent, London, W.1.
CONSUMER COUNCIL. 3 Cornwall Terrace, N.W.1.
BRITISH STANDARDS INSTITUTE. 2 Park Street, London, W.1.
COUNCIL OF INDUSTRIAL DESIGN. 28 Haymarket, S.W.1.
NATIONAL SOCIETY FOR THE PREVENTION OF CRUELTY TO CHILDREN.
   1 Riding House Street, W.1. (Central Office)
ROYAL SOCIETY FOR THE PREVENTION OF ACCIDENTS. 52 Grosvenor
   Gardens, S.W.1.
FIRE PREVENTION ASSOCIATION. Aldermary House, Queen Street,
   London, E.C.4.
THE ROYAL YACHTING ASSOCIATION. 171 Victoria Street, London,
   S.W.1.
THE BUILDING CENTRE. 26 Store Street, London, W.C.1.
CENTRAL COUNCIL FOR THE DISABLED. 34 Eccleston Square,
   S.W.1.
THE INSTITUTE OF ELECTRICAL ENGINEERS. Savoy Place, London,
   W.C.2.